The Historic New Orleans Collection
Monograph Series
ROBERT D. BUSH, General Editor

MEMOIRS
OF MY LIFE

Official seal of the colonial prefect

Published for the Historic New Orleans Collection by the
Louisiana State University Press
Baton Rouge and London

MEMOIRS OF MY LIFE

to My Son During the Years
1803 and After, Which I Spent
in Public Service in Louisiana
as Commissioner of the French
Government for the Retrocession
to France of That Colony and
for Its Transfer to the
United States

by Pierre Clément de Laussat

Translated from the French, with an Introduction,
by SISTER AGNES-JOSEPHINE PASTWA,
Order of Saint Francis

Edited, with a Foreword, by ROBERT D. BUSH

Copyright © 1978 by Louisiana State University Press
All rights reserved
Manufactured in the United States of America
Designer: Albert Crochet
Type face: VIP Palatino
Typesetter: The Composing Room of Michigan, Inc.
Printer and Binder: Kingsport Press, Inc., Kingsport, Tennessee

LIBRARY OF CONGRESS CATALOGING IN PUBLICATION DATA

Laussat, Pierre Clément de, 1756–1835.
  Memoirs of my life to my son during the years 1803 and after, which
I spent in public service in Louisiana as Commissioner of the French Government for the retrocession to France of that colony and for its transfer
to the United States.

  (The Historic New Orleans Collection monograph series)
  Translation of Memoires de ma vie.
  Bibliography: p.
  Includes index.
  1. Laussat, Pierre Clément de, 1756–1835. 2. Colonial administrators—
France—Biography. 3. Colonial administrators—Louisiana—Biography.
4. Louisiana—History—1803–1865—Sources. I. Title:

Memoirs of my life to my son... II. Series: Historic New Orleans Col-
lection. The Historic New Orleans Collection. The Historic New Orleans
Collection Monograph series.
F374.L26 1977   976.3'04'0924 [B]   77-12113
ISBN 0-8071-0365-9

Contents

Illustrations

Foreword

ARCHIVAL MATERIALS concerning the successive transfers of Louisiana in 1803 (Spain to France, then France to the United States) have been found, for the most part, in two locations: first, in the national depositories of the respective governments involved and, second, among the memoirs and private papers of the actual participants. The *Mémoires* of Pierre Clément de Laussat (1756–1835), French colonial prefect and commissioner for Louisiana, offer a great deal more than just "French views" on the Louisiana Purchase. Translated into English and published in Louisiana for the first time, they describe in detail the events of 1803 in a much larger context. Living conditions, personality conflicts, institutional patterns, modes of dress, local cuisine, labor relations, manufacturing and agricultural techniques, transportation problems, the issue of slavery, and intimate family portraits—all pass in review before the reader.

The extensive notes provide yet another source of firsthand information from the very personal remembrances of Laussat during the hectic days of Louisiana's changing sovereignty. Laussat was the last representative of a foreign power to exercise authority as a colonial administrator in Louisiana. His remembrances, observations, and marginal notes constitute primary historical source materials, and they tell us much about both the Louisiana Purchase and Laussat the man.

The Laussat Papers, of which these *Mémoires* are a part, comprise over six hundred items, with documents in French, Spanish, and English. Several institutions in Louisiana have materials in their collections pertaining to Pierre Clément de Laussat. The Special Collections Division of the Tulane University Library has several official proclamations that he issued in his capacity as colonial prefect between November 30 and December 20. Tulane also has a copy of the 1831 French limited edition of Laussat's *Mémoires sur ma vie*, as well as a typed English translation of the memoirs done in 1940 by Henri Delvile de Sinclair, though the typed copy does not have any additional annotations. The Louisiana Division of the New Orleans Public Library also has some documents from the Laussat administration. The Archival Department of the Louisiana State Museum similarly has materials regarding Laussat, and a great number of sources on the Louisiana Purchase.

The acquisition of the archival treasure known as the Laussat Papers by the Historic New Orleans Collection in 1975 was made possible by several people. Sister Agnes-Josephine Pastwa, translator of this volume, first discovered the papers. She in turn persuaded their owner, a descendant of Laussat, Antoine du Pré de Saint-Maur, of Pau, France, to share them with those in America who wished to know more about the events of 1803. Dr. Isabel French, of the Louisiana Historical Society, first introduced Sister Pastwa to the Historic New Orleans Collection and assisted in several ways toward the publication of these *Mémoires*. The Kemper and Leila Williams Foundation assumed the initiative in acquiring the Laussat Papers, thereby returning to Louisiana the several hundred documents relevant to the state's history. Mr. and Mrs. Ernest C. Villeré, in particular, played an important role in handling the final negotiations for the return of these documents to the United States. Several interested New Orleanians, including Sidney L. Villeré, Henry C. Pitot, Robert G. Pollack, and Mrs. Edwin X. de Verges, contributed information regarding the names of Louisiana residents referred to by Laussat. The advice and encouragement of Stanton M. Frazar, director of the Historic New Orleans Collection, helped bring this project to fruition. Randi de la Guéronnière carefully typed the manuscript and assisted in proofreading. Renée Peck and Mathé Allain also helped in proofreading.

As with any historical memoirs, those of Laussat must be examined with a consideration of all the personal strengths and weaknesses of the author. The data contained here will have to be compared with additional sources before a more nearly complete and authoritative history of the momentous events surrounding Louisiana and the young American republic reveals itself. This collection of documents fills one of the important gaps among the historical enigmas that plague this era.

Many of the mechanical difficulties in translating these *Mémoires* are fully explained by the translator in her introduction; however, some points need clarification here. First, Laussat was a phonetic speller, and second, his handwriting was atrocious. The surnames of several Louisianians required proper identification. Further, Laussat's entries were formally referred to only as "M." plus the surname. Throughout the *Mémoires*, where possible, proper identification of the subject has been made by use of brackets for the correct name, with Laussat's own spelling allowed to stand from that point on. Both the full spellings of French titles and their abbreviations have been retained, along with other inconsistencies in names, spellings, and descriptions, in order to preserve the authentic character and historical accuracy of the narrative. In this way, the readability of the narrative can be maintained without repetitious insertions. In the case of differences in syntax between the manuscript and the *Mémoires* published in 1831, the translator has followed the former.

The abundance of cognates in French and English gives the false appearance that translation from one to the other is a relatively simple task; however, both languages have their own very exacting nuances. When, as in this case, the original describes cosmopolitan and local customs, institutions, and history, while relating details concerning the Louisiana Purchase, translation becomes a herculean task. Although the translater has chosen to use the past tense throughout, particular dialogues and personal comments in which the French narrative present and the English are in agreement have been translated accordingly.

As Sister Pastwa explains in her introduction, the *Mémoires* do not constitute a diary or daily journal, even though they have chronological marginal notes. They are a compilation of subjects taken from Laussat's Journal, copies of correspondence sent and received while he was acting in his official capacity, and personal reminiscences made several years later. The *Mémoires* themselves, in the two manuscript volumes translated here, were then compiled and edited during the 1820s. Finally, in 1831, they were published in French in a limited edition of one hundred copies in Laussat's native city of Pau.

The extensive number of notes made by Laussat in his Journal offer much additional information not contained in the *Mémoires* and not found among the Laussat Papers at the Historic New Orleans Collection. A portion of these have been gathered by the translator and included as endnotes. A few passages that Laussat deleted from the 1831 version have also been included in endnotes in order to illustrate what he decided not to say. Laussat's brief interpolations in parentheses have been retained; brackets indicate editorial interpolations, which clarify references or correct errors in the original text.

Agnes-Josephine Pastwa is amply qualified to undertake this translation project. Her doctoral studies at Laval University in Canada involved extensive archival research on the nineteenth-century literary figure Alfred de Vigny. Her pursuit of that subject led her to manuscript sources in Pau. Her long residence in Pau, among the manuscripts used by Laussat himself to compile his *Mémoires*, provided her with a deep understanding of the Béarn region and its peculiar colloquialisms.

The arrival of the Laussat Papers in Louisiana and this publication series are manifestations of the sense of commitment by Louisianians to develop a fuller awareness of their history. In the case of the Laussat Papers, the political and cultural ties are to France, and constitute part of the long Franco-American tradition of interaction and cooperation. Laussat himself, enthusiastically approaching his new position in

Louisiana prior to its sale by France to the United States, simply overstated what he believed was obvious: "All Louisianians are Frenchmen at heart!"

ROBERT D. BUSH

Introduction

PIERRE CLÉMENT, baron de Laussat, was born in Pau on November 23, 1756, of a distinguished lineage in the province of Béarn. During the course of his career, he was both appointed and elected to several positions in the French government. He was designated as a Knight of St. Louis and was awarded the Legion of Honor medal in recognition of his devoted service.

Pierre Clément de Laussat was the son of Jean-Gratien de Laussat, lord of the château of Bernadets and of Maucor, a secular abbey of St. Castin. He served as secretary to the king and treasurer of the Crown of Navarre as well as chairman of the representative assembly in the province of Béarn. Pierre Clément's mother was Jammes-Joséphine d'Augerot, daughter of a member of the *parlement* (law court) of Pau, a town within the province of Béarn. Laussat's formal education was directed toward law. However, a royal edict of March, 1784, created an intendancy (a royal administrative district prior to 1789) from Pau to Bayonne, and he was named receiver-general of finances for a local assembly in Béarn, one of the geographical areas within this intendancy. Laussat served in this capacity until the French Revolution abolished the institution.

During the first days of the Revolution, the city of Pau appointed Laussat as its envoy to seek repeal of a law that had transferred the seat of the department (an administrative district in France *after* 1789) from Pau to the nearby town of Oloron-Ste. Marie. He went to Paris and successfully completed this task. Because Laussat was a philosophical liberal during the Revolution, his career fluctuated with the several changes in political institutions between 1789 and 1799; however, the seizure of power by General Napoleon Bonaparte and others in November of 1799 offered him new career opportunities. Laussat therefore took an active part in preparing the constitution that established the form of government known as the Consulate (1799-1804), in which Bonaparte served as First Consul. As a member of the legislature, Laussat was in a position to request that he be considered for the office of colonial prefect of Louisiana.

Many Frenchmen hoped to regain Louisiana from Spain, to whom it had been ceded in 1762. One of the persons who endorsed this idea was Napoleon Bonaparte. When he was in a position of power to do so, he concluded the secret Treaty of San Ildefonso (October 1, 1800) with Spain. France regained her former colony, although settlement of the other treaty provisions and preparations to implement them occupied the next three years. The need for a French colonial administration opened the door to professional advancement for Pierre Clément de Laussat. He quickly seized the opportunity.

On August 20, 1802, Laussat was appointed by Bonaparte to go to Louisiana as its colonial prefect, the highest ranking French civilian officer there. His official party departed from France for Louisiana on January 10, 1803. However, the Louisiana Purchase (April 30, 1803) altered his mission entirely. On June 6, 1803, Bonaparte appointed Laussat to serve as commissioner of the French government for the retrocession of Louisiana from Spain to France, and then from France to the United States; but Laussat was not to learn of his new position for several months. Upon the completion of his responsibilities in Louisiana, he went to his next assignment as prefect for Martinique. He served there from 1804 until 1809, when, the island having fallen to the British, he was made a prisoner of war and sent to England. He was released in December and permitted to return to France.

Laussat assumed his duties as prefect of Antwerp on February 9, 1810. From 1812 to 1814 he functioned similarly at Jemmapes. During the Hundred Days of Napoleon's return to France from exile, in 1815, Laussat held a seat in the Chamber of Deputies.

Upon restoration of the Bourbon monarchy (1815-1830), Laussat became governor of French Guiana. There he added merit to an already distinguished public career by a loyal and efficient administration of that colony under trying circumstances. When Laussat returned to France, Louis XVIII invested him with the dignity and honors of a baronage. Fatigue and poor health had taken their toll after his years of exertion in public office. Laussat withdrew from active participation in government and retired to his château at Bernadets, where he died in 1835.

Laussat's unpublished Journal and several volumes of memoirs covering his public life attest to his efforts toward efficient administration. For ninety-five years (1835–1929), the pertinent data remained hidden in the attic of Bernadets. Not until 1929, on the eve of his wedding, when he formally inherited the estate, did Laussat's descendant, Antoine du Pré de Saint-Maur, become aware of their existence. He himself recalled the circumstances of his discovery during an interview with me in Pau in February, 1973:

> Away up in the tower of our château at Bernadets, in a sort of round attic, lay a number of dusty canvas bags piled up high. The archival materials of Pierre Clément, baron de Laussat, lay dormant in those sacks since his death in 1835! On opening them, I felt as though I were Lord Carnarvon discovering the mummy of the Egyptian pharaoh Tutankhamen! A very pungent odor of Cayenne pepper, which Laussat had obtained from Guiana while governor there from 1819 to 1823, rose to my nostrils. All those documents so well preserved—some of them dating from as far back as the first part of the eighteenth century—had been protected against rodents and insects of every kind, which might well have destroyed them forever! As I pulled out, dusted off, and sorted that ton and a half or so of documents, each one carefully folded over several times, the history of the Laussat branch of my family, from the seventeenth century on, was revealed to me little by little.

Most exciting, however, was my own accidental discovery of Laussat's unedited Journal in 1972, which had been gathering dust on its obscure corner shelf for over a century and a half along with several oversized books and charts. These four folio volumes measured 8½ by 11 inches bound and were written on paper of various sizes and quality. Laussat refers constantly to the collection of notebooks as "cahiers de mon journal." They provide new sources of documentation and testimony regarding Laussat's political career.

From this Journal then, rich with notes and observations by Laussat and others, the former colonial prefect sifted material for his *Mémoires* published in 1831. In fact, the purpose of the *Mémoires* is stated succinctly on the first page of the Journal, which bears the imposing title "Mission Politique à la Louisiane, la Martinique et la Guyanne en 1803 et Années Suivantes." Because of the several deletions, the published *Mémoires* are far more restricted as to content and consequently less interesting than the Journal. They were compiled in two parts; Part One of the *Mémoires* consists of six books. They each contain between 180 and 198 pages of Laussat's script and describe the years from his birth to his retreat at Bernadets as baron de Laussat. These books contain a gap between 1802 and 1804, which is filled in by two separate manuscript volumes labeled Part Two—for our purpose, the most valuable part of the entire collection. The contents of this part are:

BOOK ONE: (January, 1803 to December, 1803)—200 pages of script. Contents: departure from Helvoët-Sluys; life in colonial Louisiana; the announcement of the Louisiana Purchase by the United States.

BOOK TWO: (December, 1803 to July, 1804)—198 pages of script. Contents: an extended trip up and down the Mississippi river; the participation as commissioner for the double ceremonies of the retrocession of Louisiana from Spain to France, and its cession by France to the United States; secret departure for Martinique.

Laussat originally intended to publish all eight books, but their bulk and the cost of publication induced him to publish only that section that would justify his conduct in Louisiana. In fact, this is precisely what he states in the preface to Book One of the abridged manuscript: "I recall them [those days] faithfully here, just as I have recorded them in the journal that I have kept of them. My purpose for this publication is to defend myself against all false allegations or interpretations, at such times especially when my principles and character were often opposed."

The first draft of Laussat's *Mémoires* was begun in 1821, while he was governor of French Guiana. They were carefully reworked the following year. Then he reedited them several more times before their publication in 1831. The published volume did not enjoy great success in 1831, yet excerpts from the *Mémoires* do occur frequently in volumes of Louisiana studies.

Laussat's Louisiana *Mémoires* are written on durable linen paper that still has the original écru tint and that for a century and a half has withstood climate and insect damage. Aside from a few frayed edges, the pages are in fine condition. They are tied together with heavy gray linen thread, one-half inch wide, laced through a crude perforation made two inches from the lower left corner of each page. The last few sheets of Book One show water damage, but the india ink is still black.

In order to present only the truth as Laussat saw it, the Journal as well as numerous other letters and documents were consulted. This process also helped to clarify certain facts that would otherwise seem incomprehensible or incomplete to a modern reader. In many instances, Laussat's deletions are so heavily marked out with black ink that they have become totally illegible. There are bold scrappings of passages, sometimes entire episodes, that might have presented facts in a clearer light; but they are replaced by short, bone-dry statements. Several additional sources that I referred to have been cited in the notes.

Laussat himself made no attempt to divide the contents of his manuscript into chapters. He merely set down facts, intended primarily for use by his family, in chronological order on sheets of paper six by eight inches, folded through the middle. The right half of each page he covered with his script; the other half of the page he left blank for notes, dates, paragraph headings, and corrections. Occasionally his paragraphs are involved and tortuous to read. They often contain long, digressive sentences with vague antecedents, though accumulations of short sentences also occur, producing a disagreeable, almost jerky effect to the modern reader. His Béarnais background frequently comes through in phrases like: "Je me concerte dans mon cabinet," or "Il se donnait pour la famille," and again, "promener la galerie." He shuttles verb tenses in his narration, going from the present tense to the past and then back again. Thus, in my translation, I have taken some liberties with tense in order to provide a smoother sounding prose.

Written entirely in the first person, the *Mémoires* uses a style that is simple, even mediocre in places. Certain passages lack unity; the unpretentious vocabulary lacks color; the script, at times, reveals his moods—fine and smooth when he is relaxed and content, but almost undecipherable when he is upset. Hidden emotions, ambitions, frustrations, disappointments, and a profound distrust of the men who outmaneuvered him are revealed. Laussat emerges as a lonely figure, without real political leverage and without the instruments of power.

Inaccuracies, incongruities, exaggerations, and some prejudicial remarks can sometimes be attributed to Laussat's lack of information. But he also must be charged, at times, with becoming too personally involved in his work, often imprudently, to pass unbiased judgment. However well-meaning he intended to appear, his ambivalence toward Americans and his anti-Spanish bias were unjustifiable for a person in his official position. Yet he was caught in an unenviable position between shifty Spanish officials and shrewdly calculating, even brazen, American leaders.

I do not mean to imply that Laussat's *Mémoires* were based upon unreliable or questionable sources, and therefore have little value. Whenever he was not himself involved in the course of events, he sought to correlate his personal observations with such factual information as was available to him. Laussat used the *Jamaica Gazette*, the *Moniteur*, the *Telegraph*, and the *Gazette gouvernementale de la Nouvelle-Orléans*, among others. In addition, his Journal is a meticulous record of names, dates, vessels, officers, cargoes, weather conditions, summaries of letters sent and received, and bits of political news gathered from transients visiting him in New Orleans. An amazing amount of valuable factual information is contained in thirty pages of a census report that he compiled while visiting planters and small farmers residing along the Mississippi and bayous. Added to these sources of information are several others: memoirs, questionnaires, travel accounts, charts, and records submitted at his request by knowledgeable pioneers and prominent citizens of Louisiana. All these sources of information had their purpose: "I go into these details," he wrote, "so that our families, for whom this Journal is intended, may have an idea of the kind of life we were leading."

No doubt, in the process of preparing this edition, we may have neglected some identifications, amplifications, and correlations. Trying neither to suppress nor to distort any facts, and adhering closely to Laussat's original manuscript copy of his *Mémoires*, the present study may be useful to researchers. Every effort has been made to supply identification of persons Laussat refers to by their surnames only. These identifications appear in brackets in their first appearance in the narrative; thereafter, the names are given only as Laussat himself wrote them.

AGNES-JOSEPHINE PASTWA

Acknowledgments

DURING MY YEARS of research in preparing this volume for publication, my debt of gratitude has become imposing. I shall never be able to sufficiently thank Antoine du Pré de Saint-Maur for his help and encouragement. Without his unstinting cooperation the task could not have been accomplished. Nor can I measure my gratitude to Madame de Saint-Maur, who spent many hours deciphering, discussing, and translating the difficult script. She corrected errors and helped me in a hundred different ways. I am most grateful to these two very fine people for their hospitality during my years of study and residence in Pau. Their son Nicholas helped me to translate the difficult passages containing nautical expressions; and, the viscount d'Origny, cousin of Antoine du Pré de Saint-Maur, came to Pau from Paris in order to share with me his family documents and albums. I am grateful to Alice de Columbi, descendant of Lysis de Laussat, and to the countess Hèléne de Bar de la Garde, a granddaughter of Laussat's daughter Sophie, who allowed me to read her family papers.

Many people in addition to those from the Laussat family rendered substantial aid to me in the preparation of this book. Jacques de Laprade, conservator of the Château Henri IV in Pau at the time, offered valuable guidance and encouragement. Both he and his wife assisted me as often as I needed. Eric Lavasseur of Pau spent several hours helping with the financial reports found in Book Two. Reverend Charles Bense, a native Béarnais, generously explained and translated Béarnais expressions found in the text. Hélène Lavignotte of Biarritz assisted by proofreading the translation. Sisters Joan Rutz and Mary Alonzo, together with Gary Solecki, helped unstintingly with the typing. I acknowledge with great pride my debt to Thomas Ashley, senator from Ohio; James Domengeaux of Lafayette, Louisiana; Cecil Taylor, chancellor of Louisiana State University; Samuel Wilson, Jr., associate of the Louisiana Historical Society; and Dr. Isabel French, editor and archivist for the Society. Similarly, special acknowledgment is due to Mrs. Edwin X. de Verges of New Orleans. Recognition is due also to the staff at the Cabildo in New Orleans for permission to photograph the room in which the treaty of transfer was signed. The library staffs of the Louisiana State Museum archives and the Louisiana State University in Baton Rouge were both equally helpful. Sidney L. Villeré of New Orleans assisted in verifying many of the Louisiana names mentioned in the *Mémoires*.

But most particularly, I acknowledge my gratitude to the governing body of my religious affiliation, the Order of Saint Francis, for permission to pursue this work to its conclusion, for time away from other duties, and for the overall support given me throughout the years of research involved in this project.

MEMOIRS
OF MY LIFE

Preface

THE FIRST FORTY-SEVEN years of my life in France were spent under the vigilant eyes of my compatriots and contemporaries; they were thus best able to understand and judge them.

The years that followed were employed in high positions in Louisiana, Martinique, and Guiana, where war and distance kept me isolated.

Today [August 1, 1831, at Bernadets, some fifteen kilometers from Pau], I recall them faithfully here, just as I have recorded them in the Journal that I have kept of them.

My purpose for this publication is to defend myself against all false allegations or interpretations, at such times especially when my principles and my character were often opposed.

BOOK ONE
January to December, 1803

HAVING BEEN APPOINTED, at my own request, colonial prefect of Louisiana in 1802, I said farewell to the emperor and left Paris for Rochefort on the first of December, together with my wife and my three daughters.[1]

The French expedition, for which I acted as precursor, was supposed to sail from Helvoët-Sluys in Holland.[2] The brig *Surveillant*, on the other hand, was sent from Lorient to take me aboard.[3] It was delayed. The forty days during which I was detained in the port of my embarkation seemed excessively long to me.[4] But I used this time profitably to acquire what information was offered me about this maritime theater.

On the tenth of January, the ship had finally completed preparations and slipped out to sea. It lay waiting for us in the Basque roadstead [the Île d'Aix], where a schooner transported us.[5] We embarked and I began a new destiny.

I undertook my first sea voyage somewhat late in life and with a family.[6] Twenty-one other passengers came with me. In addition, this small brig of thirty-two guns commanded by Captain Girardais had on board three staff officers, three students, a health officer, a harbormaster, and eighty crewmen.[7]

How did we ever fit in? To us—father, mother, and daughters—the captain politely relinquished his own cabin and we crowded into it: my wife on the bunk, I in an English hammock, and our children on mattresses.[8] Each night they suspended two rows of hammocks six feet overhead, wherever there was space. Not a corner could be found where men were not packed one on top of another like sardines; nor was the tiniest nook available where a man might withdraw to enjoy a moment of privacy or meditation. Seasickness troubled my wife throughout the entire crossing more than it did anyone else on board. Luckily I escaped being sick because, at the slightest symptom, I used to dash up on deck and, regardless of the weather, pace up and down in the open air.

January 15   We had been commissioned to take on board ship at Santander some 600,000 piastres fortes [colonial currency worth about one dollar each] and unload them at Saint-Domingue [Santo Domingo] on our way. At the end of five days, we reached Santander, our first port of call.[9] Here we moored on January 15. On the morning of the sixteenth, I nearly

January 16   drowned. A sudden storm had come up during the night and the waves became unusually rough. M. Ranchoud, commissioner of French commercial relations, had invited me to dinner. A boat was lowered, and it kept dashing against an iron support (in nautical terms a *"chandelle"*) projecting from the side of the brig. We flung ourselves quickly into the small boat, however, and shoved off.[10] A petty officer sent to accompany us cried out: "A leak! The boat is taking in water![11] Ahoy! A rope... a rope!" We missed it. Fortunately the longboat let down in the morning was behind us. They let us drift to it along with the current. Luckily too, our boat, its sails trimmed, listed, and though filled knee-deep with water, remained afloat. We finally reached our lifesaver, having narrowly escaped shipwreck. With the sea in such a state, even those who knew how to swim would have perished. The apprehension on board ship was great. They kept calling out to me to come back; but I did not think it was right to do otherwise than my companions in distress. I wanted to keep on going, but on persistent appeals, I returned. I found my wife just recovering from a swoon. I reassured her. I made her realize what a demoralizing effect it would have on all aboard if, for so minor an incident, I appeared frightened and backed down from our plan. So, once more I got back into the boat, and this time we reached land, after battling the winds for a half hour. Our transfer of piastres detained us from eight to ten days.

We received a warm welcome. I met some wealthy Frenchmen whom I had known before in Bilbao, young men starting out on their careers. Feasts, *tertulias*, balls, and entertainment of every kind were lavished upon us.[12] Two members of the military staff—the provisional commander of the city and his brother-in-law, M. de Miranda, major of the battalion— set the tone for the social gathering. Major Miranda was typical of the Spanish military. In the morning he made his round of visits to the lovely ladies. Rumor had it that he was in love with Mademoiselle P____. I do not know if it was true, but whenever she sang or played on the piano, he accompanied her on the guitar. And if she danced, he strummed the instrument, which he laid aside only when he left the orchestra pit for the dance floor. He used to make a pretty fuss over little things when in the company of ladies; for this, he was unanimously acclaimed as a charming gentleman. At the *tertulia*, we heard a famous guitarist; only in Spain do they know how to produce music from such an instrument.

The middle-class Spaniards hardly made a secret of their dissatisfaction with the government; their wish for revolution was rife. Certainly, it was not the fault of the bishop, Don Raphaël Mendés de Loarca, who neither liked nor approved of our own revolution. He spent his pious life in retreat, in study, in correspondence, and in the very limited society of a few little-known devout persons. His usual talk revolved around religion. There was no parish in his diocese about which he was not thoroughly informed to the least domestic details. He opposed gambling and entertainments. He had often displayed a stubborn opposition even to the wishes of the court, thus gaining quite a reputation. Fundamentally, he was a fanatical priest with a meticulous mind and was more suited to be a fourteenth-century monk than a nineteenth-century bishop.

I have sketched his portrait to show what, in general, Spanish bishops were like then [1803]. He confided in a priest from whom I learned these details. This latter put on philosophic airs and evinced indignation against a mandate of the former bishop of La Rochelle opposing the concordat and the French government.[13] The Spanish bishop and the canon give an idea of what the Iberian church was like at the time and explain its conduct ever since.

Twenty years before the close of the eighteenth century, Santander was a mere market town. Traffic in woolen exports was carred on through Bilbao, which it made prosperous. To punish Bilbao for its insistence upon privileges, the court placed high customs duties on the Biscay border and lightened those of Santander, which at the same time was declared a port *habilitado*, that is, one entitled to privileges of round-trip expeditions between the mother country and its colonies. Before long this latter town felt its advantages; it grew and flourished. It was a bustling center, and each day it gained more territory along the bay. Meat was expensive there. People spoke only Spanish, not Basque.

The mountains that separate the Asturias from Biscay are called the Montañas. These rugged, snow-covered escarpments, inhabited by bears and wolves, separate the Basque region from Galicia. At one time Pelagius [a medieval rebel about whom there seems to be confusion on Laussat's part] hid deep within their interior with what was left of the Spanish army defeated by the Moors, in order to emerge again one day and reconquer the country from them. These mountains are described as *los grandes*. The Asturians refer to each other as *montañeros*, and they call the Biscayans *provincianos*.

The street dress of the women is the *mantilla* and the *saya* [a long, full skirt]; the dress worn by the country people is an ancient Spanish costume called the *chupa y montera* [coat and cap]. The bourgeois class wears French-style clothes. The cloak is not as common as formerly; the *rondilla* [sic] is quite rare. Upon meeting, people no longer greet each other as they used to do in my younger days with "baya V. M. con Dios; guarde Dios à V. M." [God be with you; God keep you]. The word *adios* has been replaced all over Spain by the Basque word *agur*. [Laussat is obviously mistaken here.]

A lady, seeing us looking at the religious pictures, scapulars, and holy water fonts that decorated the room of one of her friends, remarked, "Well! Well! This poor woman believes in all this nonsense." These observations occupied our leisure without, however, abating in the least my burning impatience to be on my way.

Our treasure was finally loaded, and on the twenty-second of January we reembarked.[14] The weather was nasty, and the southwesterly winds were contrary. On January 23, a cannon shot signaled all laggards aboard, but the alternating southwesterly and easterly winds held us moored hopelessly until the twenty-fifth when we weighed anchor. A few straggling passengers were still ashore, but three cannon shots hurried them on. They joined us at the entrance of the channel, and at noon we passed Cape Major and were on our way. *January 23*

Four days later, we waved to Cape Ortegal, the last stretch of European mainland, and we were in the open sea. We reached the first of the great milestones into which I divided our voyage. Pau, my native city, is about half a degree more to the south than Cape Ortegal. The fleets of Tyre did not come so far, and those of London have hardly begun to appear there.

Our trip was becoming more pleasant. We all stood on deck, breathing deeply and recovering our cheerfulness, though the cold was still penetrating. Legions of porpoises escorted us, and every day we saw sailing vessels in the distance.

On the second of February, we touched at the Azores, off Sainte-Marie, the southernmost of these islands and the second milestone of our voyage. In four days the sea—now stormy, now superb—brought us to the region of flying fish and tropical climate. But on the eighth day of February and the days that followed, the ocean became placid as a mirror, the skies turned azure, and not a breath of breeze blew. The rudder was left adrift and the ship pirouetted by itself while every eye scanned the horizon for signs of cloud formations that would forecast a shower for which everybody hoped— a wish that constantly came up in conversation. Such is the picture of a calm at sea. The air was hot, the sunrise and *February 2* sunset brilliant, and the moonlight beautiful. The hours seemed eternal, and reading was the most pleasant of consolations.

One must become a sailor early in boyhood to become accustomed to the ocean's caprices and to the monotonous shipboard existence in which each life is always commingled with those of others. In those deserts suspended between water and sky, what a pleasure it is to surround oneself with the memory of people who, from their end of the world, follow us in thought and seek us out in space!

February 10   These reflections were aroused by all that I was seeing and experiencing, when the tenth of February arrived and we were forced to undergo the ransom and dull burlesque of the ceremony known as "crossing of the line" [crossing the Tropic of Cancer, northern boundary of the torrid zone].

February 24   On the morning of February 24, 1803, we encountered the coasts of the island of Saint-Domingue. The crossing was not bad. The last days were an intermingling of winds more variable than is usual in these climates. We dropped anchor early on the morning of the twenty-seventh in the harbor of the Cape [Français], not far from the ship *Admiral Latouche-Treville*. We had reached the third milestone.

It was very hot. I was writing with only a shirt on. Saint-Domingue is a mountainous mass. One might say that Mount Pelion was piled on Ossa and that we were facing the battlefield of the Titans.[15] Behind the first range we perceived, like a cloud, the mountain of Cibao. From it, Columbus brought back to Spain in 1493 the first grain of gold ore, which has since cost the peoples of the New World so dearly. Beyond La Grange one could see Monte Cristo, one of the settlements established by Columbus.

The colonial prefect, Daure, sent me some oranges, naseberries, mangoes, and bananas—all indigenous fruits of the equator with which I became acquainted and which are not nearly so good as the peaches, pears, and apples from my locality [in the Basque country].

The situation of our army was deplorable. It acknowledged Negroes as masters, even down to the city gates.[16] My attention was drawn to their camps, their fires, and their signals on the plantations of Duplàa, Vaudreuil, etc., which were reduced to ruin. During the entire forty-eight hours of our layover, they pillaged, slaughtered, and devastated the small isle of La Tortue and massacred its proprietor [Jean-Baptiste] Labatut, a descendant of the family of the original land holders. Very strict orders from the minister prevented us from going ashore. We departed from these desolate coasts on the twenty-seventh of February, slowly hugging the fringe of the island, to the noise of cannon and gunfire, and in the glowing light of huge piles of fagots from which thick, curling smoke rose here and there along the shore.

From there we directed our course along the island of Cuba, often being no farther than three leagues from its coast and easily distinguishing its unusual vegetation and its extensive wooded areas. Frequent calms thwarted us. During the daytime the heat was unbearable; but the nights were delightful. The heavenly bodies have a far greater brilliance here than in Europe—the moon is paler and the stars more luminous. Their scintillating lights added a new charm to the coolness of the air, so pleasant to inhale after a day of sweltering heat.

The endless calms were succeeded by a typical stiff breeze *March* that gave us hope of eventually coming out from this inter- *4* minable channel between Cuba, where we recognized Santiago, founded by Columbus, and Xayamaca (Jamaica), where he was shipwrecked in 1494 near the very places that we were now sighting and where, had it depended upon the jealousy of the Spanish governor, he would have died forgotten. It was from this place that he wrote the king of Spain the letter in which he described the grief that penetrated his very soul, less because of misfortune than ingratitude.

The slack in our speed exhausted the supply of fresh food, not for our table, but for the table of the ship's crew; and our entire water supply was polluted. I had brought along two Smith and Cuchet filter canteens. They were used at the captain's table and by the end of three weeks had lost their efficacy. They essentially made use of charcoal. Our chemist,

Blanquet, said that it was a common practice. He and the engineer [Antoine Joseph] Vinache planned to give it a try. They lined the bottom of a barrel with canvas and a thick layer of powdered charcoal, over which they poured a heavy layer of sand. They needed to pour a great deal of water over it to wash it; fresh water being unavailable, they used salt water. The polluted water used for the experiment came through the filter pure, but the fresh water emerged salty. Discouraged by the contradictions and the jibes to which they were subjected, the chemist gave up the effort and the engineer persisted alone. Using rain water and such other water as he could scrounge up, he drew from his improvised filter water that was at first barely palatable and then some that was very good. We stopped drinking water that was polluted and reeked of sulphur. The famous cask was given the place of honor on deck. Everyone came to draw water from it, and they all praised Vinache for his persevering efforts. The processes of purifying water and of disinfecting the air by means of fumigation, according to the method of Guyton de Morveau, were the two marked features of our navigation; both were crowned with success.

During the night of March 6, 1803, we passed Cape Saint Antoine at the western extremity of the island of Cuba without even being aware of it. And thus we passed the final milestone of our boring voyage and were in the Gulf of Mexico. The short, deep waves indicated this. The ship's movements became more abrupt here and fatigued its passengers even more. Bad weather is rare here; lulls and storms are frequent during June, July, and August.

March 16 and 17   What a magnificent night! A brilliant full moon with a pearly luster appeared toward the east, while the sun, surrounded by purple clouds, concealed its fiery globe on the horizon. A cool breeze from the southwest filled our sails. Our brigantine ploughed the waters swiftly at three leagues an hour. Sirius, Canope, the eye of Taurus, and Gemini blended their dazzling rays with the sheets of light in which the moon enveloped the skies, and which seemed to spread out and undulate on the surface of the sea. Over and

over again we spoke of our approaching face-to-face meeting
with the Father of Waters.

Frigate bird, that swallow of the ocean, which, like the
wind, with a light wing skims the water and then, like the
eagle, soars above the clouds from which it swoops down
again toward the sea and returns triumphantly carrying a fish
in its beak—that frigate bird had come the day before and
again that day toward nightfall, to repeat the favorable au-
gury of our voyage. "Frigate bird, the sight of which brings
joy to the heart of navigators, would that I could send you as a
messenger today," I cried out, "to my friends in Europe to let
them share the serene tranquility of these waters."

Two trees that the Mississippi River carried along with it
down to the Gulf of Mexico brushed the sides of our ship this
morning. We again crossed the Tropic of Cancer. But the sky *March 9*
changed, and a thick cloud spread far on the distant shore. It
moved us away from the land we were about to touch. We
knit our brows. Here we were nearly in port and then were
driven back. What bad luck! Flocks of birds urged us in vain
to come and share the security of their nests; trees, large and
small, announced in vain the proximity of the Mississippi. *March 10*
We retreated and pulled back some twenty-five leagues from
its mouth. What good does it do to hear them call out,
"Land"? "Italiam... Italiam" [phrase used by mariners in
Virgil's *Aeneid* upon sighting their homeland Italy]. The color
of the sea had changed. We sounded twenty fathoms and
sighted by telescope the tower at La Balise. [17] We moored. We *March 11*
were leeward! We weighed anchor at midnight and tacked
southward; but the currents gained on us, and we dropped
more and more leeward. The weather became foul and the
seas very high. The sails were trimmed and furled. The hori- *March 13, 14 and 15*
zon was misty, and there was rain, strong winds, squalls,
high, roaring waves, and water thirty-eight to forty-eight
fathoms deep. The brig rolled and pitched. No bottom at a
hundred fathoms. We were submitted to the equinoctial
storms; however, in all this, we ran no danger that would
allow me to embellish my story with exaggerated descriptions. The prolonged and deafening noise of the sea; the im-

pact of the waves as they broke against the sides of the frail vessel; their sudden and furious eruptions as high as the tops of the sails, from which they fell back in torrents that flooded the deck; and the distant whistling of the north wind at intervals—this was our most distressing situation, mainly because of its duration and the proximity of the coast. It was difficult to sleep, our slumber being continually interrupted by the violent jolting of the ship and the noise of the rigging and the sea. I was especially preoccupied for my wife, who could not quite refrain from indulging in nostalgic thoughts. Yet she never expressed any regrets. But during the night between Monday and Tuesday (March 14), she could not help remarking, "Anyway, dear, it would be cruel to have come this far only to perish by such a sad death."

There prevailed on board our floating island a little bad temper and considerable misanthropy. Scarcely anyone of the passengers escaped seasickness or some indisposition amounting to the same thing. But we did not give up hope; we were at the mouth of the Mississippi. In two days, we kept telling ourselves, this trial, which fate has reserved for us on this other side of the ocean, will be forgotten.

March 17 and 18   Yet, in a hurry to move, we dropped anchor there and found ourselves still west of the channel the next morning at daybreak. We promptly made for the sea again. By what strange misfortune did we always end up in the eastern pass, between that of La Balise and that of La Loutre, and therefore in the direction of the wind?

We ran a new series of tack. We distinguished several vessels facing the shore of La Balise three or four leagues to the northwest and recognized this point perfectly, as well as La Balise itself, with its tower and buildings. We headed straight for it, and in a minute the fog settled, cleared, rose, and disappeared. The least little cloud constricted our hearts. The setting sun was rather clear, and we strained at the sails. Twilight was about to wane when we moored at last among eight ships that we could no longer distinguish in the dark.

What a good night we spent! What a peaceful sleep! We awoke leisurely and late. A heavy fog surrounded us. We heard the cries of people and the blowing of fog horns and trumpets coming from the other ships around us. Now and then the masts of vessels could be seen through the clearing fog. The winds were blowing from the northwest—impossible to enter. No matter. The river water was fresh at low tide and we drank Mississippi water. At eleven o'clock the fog disappeared. Our eight anchored companions, with their flags flying high, formed a squadron around us. The yellow and dirty waters spread out and blended with the horizon in a narrow border scarcely visible. High atop the masts someone signaled the arrival of a longboat, which was taking soundings, setting up buoys, and moving forward. Was it an American vessel preparing to leave without a pilot? Were they fishermen's boats? No. Was the boat heading towards us? Yes! It was he! It was the pilot (Juan) Ronquillo.

Ronquillo, the chief pilot of La Balise, sent someone to fetch me in order to lodge us for the night at his house; my wife and daughters got into his boat. By a special messenger, I sent my dispatches to the Spanish governor, [Don Manuel de] Salcedo, at New Orleans.[18]

We weighed anchor. A favorable breeze propelled us ahead. The pilot perched atop the mast on a yardarm, where, crouched low with his neck stretched, eyes straining ahead, and a cigar in his mouth, he called out: "Veer to the wind . . . that's it . . . steer . . . take soundings." We saw some breakers. Two branches from a palm tree surfaced near us, and we passed over them. We heard the pilot's voice announce, "We've crossed the bar." At the same time, a covered boat arrived and a young officer, pleasant and quite handsome, wearing the epaulettes of a second lieutenant, came on board.[19] He was a wellborn Creole, officer of the Louisiana Regiment, and commander of the post. At that moment the garrison stationed there had ten men; in wartime, there were between seventeen and twenty-five. He came to see us and brought us some provisions.

March 20

Now that I was on the river, I had no reason to remain on board ship any longer. I joined my family at Ronquillo's house.[20] He had been a main helmsman when Ulloa [Spanish governor] assigned him to this post in 1763. His excellent health reassured us of the salubrity of the area. He had seen thousands of changes in the mouths of the river, which must be explored daily by taking soundings.

The houses in this settlement were constructed of wood. Upon awakening, I could see daylight through the chinks between the boards that served as walls for the room I occupied. We slept on mattresses stuffed with Spanish moss (*Tillandsia usneoïdes*). These suit the climate perfectly, owing to their resilience and coolness. During the night I complained of an irritating rash that I mistook for a fever; it was what is known as *brûlots* or *bêtes rouges*—microscopic insects of the species of mites [sand fleas], which devoured me.

March I spent the morning exploring La Balise. It contained Ron-
21 quillo's houses; quarters for sixteen student pilots; the customs house; barracks for the soldiers and officers; and a guardhouse. There was also a tower constructed of grating and latticework to cut out the wind, about forty-five feet above the ground and approximately fifty feet above the highest level of the river, with a spire in the form of a steeple, atop which a flag was raised. One can see it out on the ocean five leagues away. The view from this tower embraced the sea, some of the smaller islands, the bar, some breakers to the right and left, large spans of water (bayous), tall reeds submerged in marshes, and to the southwest, the old French fort, of which there still remained orange groves, orchards, and the ruins of the arsenal.

The soil here has no firmness; the little that is capable of some staying power is reclaimed. The river chews away and deepens its banks on one side while it forms and builds them up on the other. Its banks bristle with trees carried along by the waters and haphazardly entangled with one another. In this way it enlarges its delta each year, a little at a time. Of its four passes—the one on the southwest, the one on the south, that of La Loutre, and the one at La Balise on the east—only the last one is navigable. The more the river floods, the shallower the pass.

We returned aboard ship about noon.[21] At one o'clock, the

wind being from the south, we weighed anchor but dropped it again after covering one league.

The commander of Fort Plaquemines [Fort St.-Philippe], M. [Pierre Joseph de] Favrot, sent word asking me to spend a few days at his house to rest up and offered me some fresh provisions, pastries, and apples packed in an Indian basket.[22] *March 22*

By eleven o'clock we sailed again; at three we moored. At this spot, the river measured five hundred fathoms across. The contrary wind having subsided at ten o'clock in the evening, we set sail again, and after covering three leagues, stopped. But we had sailed around the South Point and that was a great deal. The next morning, at eight o'clock, a favorable easterly wind propelled us at the rate of one league per hour in spite of the current. The river at that point is a league wide. By these minute details I hope to give an idea of the navigation on this river, which is rendered difficult and troublesome by its numerous sinuosities, the varying winds needed, and the continual atmospheric disturbances during that season. *March 23* *March 24*

Don Manuel Salcedo, a captain and eldest son of the Spanish governor, together with Don Beniño-Garcia-Calderon, a second lieutenant of the Louisiana Grenadiers, was sent by the governor to assist me and to offer information I would need. We moored opposite Fort Plaquemines, where we landed. M. Favrot, an old Frenchman and loyal soldier, received us in the midst of his family. He was candor and hospitality personified. Joy beamed in this good man's face upon seeing us.

We examined the fort. Plaquemines was like a small island in the middle of the swamps. People in this region are plagued with mites and mosquitoes, and it was necessary to change the garrison frequently. Eighteen iron cannons and one fort made up the defense of the post. The commander and the soldiers cultivated a vegetable garden that called for a continual war against high water, weeds, and insects. The commander's residence was comfortable enough. Fort Bourbon, on the opposite side of the river, was armed with several iron cannons that crossfired with those of Fort Saint-Philippe.

We had an excellent dinner in a cheerful atmosphere. End-less toasts were accompanied by artillery fire and French songs with choruses praising love and wine. We had a minia-ture exhibition of life in the colonies. About five or six in the evening, we took our leave and returned to the ship.

Toward nightfall, I went aboard the Spanish governor's boat, which was manned by sixteen sailors and followed by another government launch that belonged to the intendant and was manned by ten sailors. "Pull away!" and we were off. One does not take a chance on the river at night unless one is perfectly familiar with it. One hugs its shoreline and, if the current is too strong, crosses over to the other side. All of the banks bristle with trees carried by the river. Piled one on top of the other, the trees form natural obstacles. But occa-sionally some stand upright, exposing only their tips above the surface of the water. These *chicots*, as they are called, catch the boats, we soon discovered. Fortunately, we extri-cated ourselves after an hour. It is easier to avoid these dan-gers during the day.

March 25 Daylight revealed a sheet of water some twelve to fifteen hundred fathoms wide, with numerous trees floating on the surface of the river, and with alligators, some resting peace-fully on the shore, others spilling into the water. There were thick-wooded river banks, a few miserable shacks, lush var-iegated vegetation, and no road other than the paths made by wild animals and hunters. Such was the sight on the way to the Duplessis plantation, about eleven leagues from New Orleans. Although not wealthy, the proprietor was hospita-ble.[23] He had ten mulatto children. From his house to New Orleans a system of relays set up every two leagues and maintained by dragoons assured land transportation into the city.

Resuming our navigation at noon, we landed at four o'clock at the Gentilly plantation, where we were treated with magnificent generosity. Well known for its hospitality, Gentilly is one of the fine plantations between New Orleans and the sea. Sugar and cotton are cultivated and a sawmill is operated. We dined there and spent the night.

Boarding ship again at three o'clock in the morning, we
stopped at nine o'clock for breakfast at the Sancier plantation.
The Sanciers were seven brothers, two of whom lived there.
The one who received us had married a young cousin and
had two children. They were half-wild. The husband took
great pains to prove to me that he descended from the first
French immigrants at Mobile. But it was beyond his capacity
to tell us from what part of France his ancestors had come. He
had only a general idea of Europe and France, not even distinguishing these regions, which for him contained neither
provinces nor cities. But if he was a very poor geographer, he
was an excellent hunter and did not miss a deer a hundred
paces away. He was poor, but fed a pack of hounds, and, like
all the colonists, gave generously what he had. He served us
some *café au lait*, which his little wife prepared in our presence. These half-savages did not appear healthy, with their
sallow skin and frail look. But they were all nerves.

We took to our boats once more and stopped at noon at the
Sibben [F.-J. Siben] plantation, three or four leagues from
New Orleans.[24] Carriages had been sent to fetch us. We arrived at three o'clock and within an hour we were at the
governor's gate, greeted with salvos by the artillery from the
forts. The governor was attended by the commanders, the
principal officers of the garrison, and the heads of the civil
authority. I stayed about eight minutes, seated beside him.
Then I retired to the house they had engaged for me, that of
Bernard [de] Marigny, at the east gate of the city. The governor accompanied by his officers, came to pay me a visit
shortly thereafter.

The following day, Sunday, I received the *cabildo*, or the
municipal council; [Paul] Lanusse, a Béarnais from Orthéz,
was at its head as *premier alcalde*. The clergy, three deputies of
commerce, and several residents swelled the cortege. The
next day, after a dinner to which he had invited me, the
governor took me for a ride in his carriage as far as Bayou
Saint John.[25] It was the fashionable promenade, but just the
same, quite woebegone.

The Pontalbas received us as if we were members of the

family. M. [Joseph Xavier Delfau] de Pontalba gave me some
invaluable gifts—his good reputation, the goodwill of his relatives, and the friendship of M. [Jean Baptiste] Charpin.[26] To
M. de Pontalba and to M. Charpin we owed everything.

We had, for our use, M. de Marigny's furniture, and M.
[Jacques Enould de] Livaudais' linens and slaves. M. Charpin
showed more concern for us than we could have ourselves;
he saw to everything, provided for everything, and gained for
us the goodwill of all his friends.

Once established in my post, I organized my life. Here we
were in our new country, in our new home, in the midst of
new duties. All Louisianians are Frenchmen at heart!

March 28 I began my inspections and transactions for the servicing of
our expedition upon its arrival. Quarters, hospitals, stores,
provisions—I tried to see to it that nothing escaped my attention. A proclamation, in which I made a few allusions to
O'Reilly's atrocities against the French when he took possession of the colony for Spain [1769–1770], displeased Governor
Salcedo; but it encouraged the patriotism of the colonists.[27]
Enemies of France endeavored, either through fear or
jealousy, to embitter the people, to worry them, and even to
arouse them. Sometimes they used religion, sometimes slavery. They alarmed the Anglo-Americans and the Louisianians
about their relationships. Unprincipled, penniless men
poured in from all sides. Criminally greedy traders were
bringing in Negroes from Saint-Domingue. With each day
the evil worsened. It was high time the French government
came forward and announced its rights and intentions here.

This country deserves the best administration; it offers both
great possibilities of improvement and great obstacles. I made
it known clearly that our government afforded special protection to religious worship, held principles both kind and firm
about slavery, professed a great respect for treaties, and
treated its neighbors with the consideration that makes for
good relations. Everywhere I promised impartiality and pro-
bity, support for what was good, and suppression of evil. I
expected very much from these colonists because they were a
good breed of men.

My time was taken up with trifles. Countless visits from thirty leagues around, kind attentions, courtesies and civilities, offers of furniture, offers of carriages—everything was showered upon me. I responded by unpacking my luggage little by little. The intendant [Juan Ventura] Morales lived on the best of terms with me.[28] I had reason to be well satisfied with the Spanish leaders, in spite of the etiquette and punctilious formalism from which they will never deviate.

I proceeded with a few adjudications and concluded a few transactions. I held conferences with the war commissioner, the intendant, and the *premier alcalde;* and I spent two hours with the governor.[29] I obtained permission for the French flag immediately to be treated like the Spanish flag. Since I intended to send back right away the brig that had brought me here, I was kept extremely busy preparing dispatches for France. *April 3, 4, 5, and 6*

These days of the Easter festival were devoted to the church. On Maundy Thursday, my wife was going to church in a carriage when a Negro on sentinel duty stopped her as her carriage pulled away. I hurried to register a complaint with the governor, who seemed disturbed and sent his son to check into the circumstances and settle the matter. The guilty sentinel was jailed and the duty officer imprisoned. I was satisfied with the reparation made and asked for clemency. The governor drew my attention to the fact that, in Spain, the king himself walked to church on that day and on Good Friday as well. My wife was not aware of this custom, which did not, however, excuse the insult.[30] *April 7, 8, and 9* *April 10–15*

The Marquis de Casacalvo [Casa Calvo], a brigadier of the army who was stationed in Havana, was associated with Governor Salcedo for the retrocession of Louisiana, and his impending arrival was announced.

On Easter Monday, I brought together at a banquet the governor, the intendant, the commissioner of war, the civil and military chiefs and the vice-consul of the United States. It was a return courtesy extended to the governor and the intendant. No toast was overlooked, and the guns from our ship echoed them in the distance. Frenchman that I am, I would have been ashamed not to return the courtesy to the Spaniards.

New Orleans social circles are not above small-town gossip, though there are many people. The men have a casualness about them and are very frank. They also have a singular fondness for pleasure. Their meals are intermingled with toasts and songs with traditional refrains. The women have good manners and beautiful figures. Men and women combined an extremely remarkable cleverness with natural elegance. The luxury of the wardrobe resembles that of Paris.[31]

Charpin, who came to see us several times a day, was our right arm. As one must leave the city through its less-populated section to arrive at our house, people generally departed about ten o'clock in the evening, and no one came later. Except for this, and even with it, our residence was most pleasant. The river presented a beautiful sight. We were located on the semicircle that outlined the harbor. One hundred and twenty ships—French, Spanish, and mostly Anglo-American—spread far out like a floating forest and formed a prospect worthy of the busiest regions on the earth.

April 16–19 The wind went around the compass every four or five days. Galleries along the four sides of the house provided coolness when it was hot and warded off the chill when it was cold. The noonday sun concentrated its heat on the head, like a magnifying glass. Storms, already breaking, sounded like terrible earthquakes. Although it was not more than two or three hundred steps from our house to the city, a trip to town often seemed longer because of the heat, rain, or wind. Therefore, we stayed home as if in the country, happy with our peace and quiet.

The intendant Morales, whose difficult character had made enemies, was at least incorruptible and above suspicion. Wealthy, he owed his fortune to personal speculations. As an administrator, he had talent and a keen mind. As for the rest, what a detestable policy was that of the Spanish government! What dishonest manipulation! What corruption!

I went through considerable negotiations to provide what-

ever would be needed by our expedition upon its reaching *April*
port. Mercantile enterprises here were usually limited to the *and*
sale and purchase of existing commodities, tradesmen being *May*
reluctant to expose themselves to uncertain risks. The work-
man made enough money from his labor alone, the cost of
which was excessive. At each step I encountered incredible
difficulties in my transactions; I was continually occupied
with them for two weeks and concluded only a few. I took
care of the bare necessities by having the work done
economically—the worst kind of administrative procedure
but, at the time, the lesser evil.

I sent the minister accurate reports on conditions up to the
departure of the brig *Surveillant*. I had my official messages
and those of the minister of the French navy sent to M. de
Somoruelos, the governor of Havana.[32] The brig *Surveillant*
already had my packet of letters for France. "Sine me liber
ibis." [from Ovid's *Tristia:* "You will go without me little *April*
book."] The *Surveillant* raised anchor and disappeared; and *20 and 25*
on the twenty-fifth of April, it sailed out of the Mississippi
and put to sea.

I calculated the forthcoming arrival of the expedition and *April*
continued my preparations for quartering the troops—seeing *and*
to their housing, bedding, hospitals, mosquito netting, and *May*
provisions of flour and bakery. I obtained extremely good
terms everywhere because my word was trusted. This was far
different from the practice of the government that preceded
us.

Making every effort to become well acquainted with a
country in which nothing would henceforth be alien or indifferent to me, I received people and cultivated them. I took
trips and I hurried here and there, listening, asking ques-
tions, and taking notes.

This time of the year was most interesting; the settlers
flocked in from all the posts. They called posts the establishments that were scattered in the remote areas of the colony
and formed little groups.[33] Farmers came into town to sell
their produce and purchase supplies; traders brought in local
raw materials and took back city products. People kept

abreast of the situation and gathered news from all the tribes and clans. Each day brought new faces.

M. Duvilliers [le chevalier, aîné, Couland de Villiers], son of a knight of Saint Louis and descendant of Jumonville of Canada, lived at Opelousas, where he was held in high esteem by the Indians among whom he had spent his life. He had an independent and original disposition and was eager to meet me because France was still dear to him.

April
24
The land of Romand [Jacques Etienne Roman], a planter from the same region, was covered with his herds; he raised the finest cotton in Louisiana and had grown rich after thirty-six years of work and diligence. Father Viel, a former Oratorian father from Juilly, came to see me from the neighboring territory of Atakapas.[34] He knew all our Béarnais [fellow colonials from Béarn]. He was driven back to his native country [Louisiana] by the [French] Revolution. He lived in this remote region among his own people, by whom he was much loved. Spanish fanaticism persecuted him here. I also had a visit from M. Dublanc [Louis Charles de Blanc], commander of his district.

[Auguste] Chouteau, a natural son of the younger Laclède and brother of our [Pierre] Laclède, the forest ranger, was a native of our Apse Valley [in France]. He came down from St. Louis (five or six hundred leagues), where he governed and traded.[35] The Osage Indians, who are known to be "no man's friends," are his western neighbors.

When the waters run high, it takes at least two weeks to come from St. Louis by boat, and from forty to forty-five days to go back up.[36] St. Louis was the prospective residence of the assistant prefect, M. [Charles] Maillard, who I was instrumental in having appointed to that post, as he requested.

From Pointe-Coupée came M. Podras [Julien Poydras], one of the most important and most enlightened cotton planters. He was accompanied by M. Destrehan [Jean Noël d'Estrehan] from the German Coast, the leading sugar producer in Louisiana. M. Bahen [Joseph Bahan] was born at Cette (Hérault) to a parliamentary family related to the Cambons of Toulouse. His father was one of the victims of the Revolution and his two

May

brothers served in Egypt. He had come to Louisiana while still very young, not even knowing how to write, and he spent his life in the Ouachitas region. With his simple common sense and extreme good nature, he had surer and more accurate information about the interior of the colony and about relations with the Indians than most other settlers.

[Emmanuel] Prudhomme, from Nakitoches [Natchitoches], gave me news about that old section, which has no more than 150 households.[37] They have mixed very little and are French in heart and blood. Although tobacco from Nakitoches has preserved its reputation, its cultivation has dwindled and has been taken over by that of cotton.

Having come into contact with Americans as well, I enjoyed entertaining them at my table. There were a good number of them present when M. Youngs [Samuel Young] of Pointe-Coupée, a Pennsylvanian by birth and an opulent proprietor whose family was well established, told me boldly that he had no doubt the western states would one day form a nation independent from those in the east. It was then a common opinion that one did not conceal.

While I took advantage of every occasion to extend my knowledge about the remote regions of the country, I did not neglect the environs of the city. The Livaudais family lived approximately two leagues away. Relatives of the Pontalbas and friends of M. Charpin, they joined him in showering us with attentions. Their simple manners were marked by amiability and honesty. The grandmother, the father and mother, the son and his wife and two children—four generations—all lived together in harmony. They had sixty Negroes and more than 100,000 francs of income. They were badly and humbly lodged, obviously sacrificing pleasure to utilitarian considerations.

The residence of M. [Jean-Etienne de] Borée [or Boré], two leagues ahead, on the other hand, was quite attractive, surrounded by lovely gardens with magnificent lanes of orange trees loaded with abundant blossoms as well as with fruit in every stage of ripening.[38] It was in this place that the first attempt to raise sugarcane in Louisiana was made and sustained. This cultivation is still carried out successfully there and has had, since, many prosperous imitators in the neighboring area. Eight or nine plantations separate this one from New Orleans. The river and its left-bank levee mark this distance from one end to the other.

To the eye, the levee simply looks like the ridge of one of our boundary ditches. This ridge is sufficient to hold back flood waters at road level, but dampness alone seeps through. The swelling water will rise about six inches more during the next month, yet the roads are already beginning to be gutted and bad. Moreover, they are neither raised and turtlebacked, nor macadamized, nor bordered by ditches; in a word, they are very poorly maintained.

Transportation between the country and city is carried on by an active navigation service for several hundreds of leagues. Still, no river anywhere has greater need for good towing lanes or, rather, for steamboats, so suitably invented for his country by the American Fulton.

The products of Louisiana are already quite considerable. Wherever the Anglo-Americans settle, land is fertilized and progress is rapid. There is always a group of them who act as trailblazers, going some fifty leagues into the American wilderness ahead of the settlers. They are the first to migrate to a new area. They clear it, populate it, and then push on again and again without any purpose other than to open the way for new settlers. Those who thus forge ahead into the unknown places are called black settlers [Laussat means backwoodsmen here]. They set up their temporary shanties, fell and burn trees, kill the Indians or are killed by them, and disappear from this land either by death or by soon relinquishing to a more stable farmer the land which they had begun to clear. When a score or so of such new colonists have congregated into one location, two printers arrive—one a federalist, the other an antifederalist—then the doctors, then the lawyers, and then the fortune seekers. They drink toasts, nominate a speaker, set up a town, and raise many children. Finally, they advertise the sale of vast tracts of land, attracting and deceiving as many land buyers as possible. They exaggerate the population figures so that they may quickly reach the sixty thousand souls entitled to form an independent state and be represented in Congress. And so another star appears on the flag of the United States!

A district under the Spanish or French regime might begin, end, start again, get lost again, and so successively until its fate is sealed—permanent existence or annihilation. Under the Anglo-Americans, a newly born state may thrive with more or less prosperity, but it will never decline; it keeps on growing and strengthening. One can hardly realize that forty years ago, on these vast expanses of land from the shores of the Mississippi to the Alleghenies, there was not a single farmhand to cultivate the soil. Today, these same regions flood the New Orleans market, by way of the Mississippi, with their abundant harvests.

On the other side of the river, opposite the harbor, stood the powder magazine. Should it have blown up, it would have caused great devastation in the city. Baron de Carondelet had built it on what was formerly known as the King's Plantation.[39] Apparently, it had been quite neglected. I took advantage of the visit I made there to push on as far as the contiguous plantation of Bernaudy [Bernard Bernoudy], founded by the Pradelles [Chevalier de Pradel] of the French navy. Everything here was in the French style, even the old furniture; in what remained of it, one could still recognize Parisian workmanship. No other residence in the colony was so elegant. Governor Galvés [Don Bernardo de Gálvez] of Spain used to make it his summer home.[40] The view took in the entire city. But landslides caused by the river had already gouged out an arpent of land and threatened the very building from only a few yards away.

I became familiar with the vicinity of New Orleans. On the twenty-second of May, I got into a boat at the Port du Canal Carondelet to go by way of Bayou Saint John to the fort that defends its entrance on Lake Pontchartrain. I was accompanied by M. de Salcedo's eldest son and by Vinache, the major of the corps of engineers.

The canal was an easy job. One needed only to conceive the

May 4— Powder magazine

Bernaudy plantation

May 22— Carondelet Canal, Bayou St. John, Fort, and Lake Pontchartrain

idea and to will it, as had Baron de Carondelet. The maintenance, so long as it was taken care of annually, was neither
difficult nor expensive; yet nothing had been done to it for the
last seven years. The depth, which once reached seven to
eight feet, was no longer any more than two or three feet. The
canal, just half a league in length, was very useful. This
bayou (in Louisiana they call bayous those waters which,
either from the river or from the lakes, reach like little bays or
small waterways into the land and thereby permit navigation)
extended as far as the walls of the city. The place where it
came to an end was quite scenic. A bridge spanned it. Regular
lake traffic stopped here and created a bustling harbor. Its
clear bluish water contrasted with the yellow muddy water of
the Mississippi River. A kind of small town made up of
taverns, inns, dance halls, and vauxhalls had risen on this
spot. It is the most regular goal for outings and rendezvous in
the town.

The depth of the bayou reaches almost everywhere five,
six, seven, eight, or nine feet; and there are hardly more than
two shallow spots where heavily loaded ships need to take
precautions against running aground. The halfway mark is
indicated by a tiny island forming a thick cluster of greenery
and shade. The shores are almost everywhere cypress groves,
that is, forests of cypress trees and forests of willows, having
trees that rise from the depths of the freshwater pools in
which their lower trunks are immersed.

To the right of the bayou, the plantations end at about three
hundred paces from the port. Those to the left, desolate clear-
ings sprinkled here and there with a few shabby huts, extend
much farther. Finally, after several meanderings, one reaches
its mouth; seven or eight fishermen's cabins and a small cot-
tage announce it. M. Pierre Palao [Don Pedro Palas y Pratz], a
lieutenant of the Louisiana Regiment, had his quarters here.
These particular commands are privileged posts that provide
a bonus, since the officer supplies his garrison and makes a
profit from it.

The fort was a miserable wooden bastion standing on soft
ground. It overlooked the bar, was armed with nine iron

cannons, and held a detachment of twenty to twenty-five men. The bar was no more than 2½ feet of water deep. This lake has no tide, but when the south or the southeasterly wind blows [Laussat here means northerly winds that cause the seas to rise along the south shore of Lake Pontchartrain], the sea rises along the shore five, six, seven, even eight, feet. During hurricanes, these waters have been known to inundate the fort, whose ground level is artificially raised about three feet above the surrounding land.

The bar is treacherous. Baron de Carondelet had an iron palisade constructed on either side so as to form a kind of exit canal five or six hundred feet in front of the lake. Although the plans drawn up for this project were executed, they produced little results, and some of the rotting posts were left to turn into dangerous obstacles.

Three large boats crossed the lake—one from the northeast and two others from the south, the latter two from Pensacola or from Mobile. On this side [of Lake Pontchartrain], the route leads to these latter ports by sea; on the other side, by a short-cut, it leads to Natchez and the western United States. How many ways for easy and frequent communication exist between New Orleans and the remotest regions! The more one examines this country, the more one is convinced that it is destined to become, very shortly, one of the most populated, most productive, most lively, and richest countries in the world.

Crossing the bridge of Bayou Saint John, as we did one day, one comes directly into places they call Metairie and Providence. I made this trip on horseback and came back along the river. Metairie is located inland, toward the mid-point of the territory separating the Mississippi from Lake Pontchartrain. This section had been cleared within the last few years. There one still traveled among the primeval forests of the New World—faint reflections of the immense forests in which one loses oneself more and more the deeper one penetrates the interior. Magnolia, sycamores, and live oaks of every species are found there, as well as those thousands upon thousands of trees, exotic to Europe and indigenous to

America, and thousands of tropical vines that tangle, inter-
lace, and form a thick, flexible, and swaying network across
the forest.

After 4½ leagues of riding, we emerged on the river bank
at the Sauvée [Pierre Sauvé] plantation, where we spent the
entire day. Few sugar mills are as successful. There I saw sugarcane growing out in the fields and worksheds in operation.
The return trip by way of the levee covered approximately
five leagues.

Temperature   Although the temperature was generally quite pleasant, its
variations carried it rapidly from one extreme to the other
within a space of twelve, twenty-four, or forty-eight hours.
One day may have been a real spring day; the following night
would bring a violent wind from the east and northeast, a
veritable gale with the waters of the river rising a foot. The
wind blowing throughout the day would be followed by a
fine rain such as a drizzle in May. The next day might be cold
enough to call for heat; and the day after tropical. One
perspired continuously and remained in a sweat even while
sitting in an armchair. A storm would break out, bringing
twelve to eighteen hours of relief. The mornings, however,
were for the most part delightful. Such was May in Louisiana.
We were to see what the summer months, about which
people frightened us, were like.

May 10—   The Marquis de Casacalvo of Havana, a brigadier general in
Marquis de   the Spanish armies, whom the Madrid cabinet had assigned
Casacalvo   to M. de Salcedo, governor for the retrocession of Louisiana,
landed in the city on May 10, 1803, with his second son, a
child of fourteen who was a cadet in a regiment. The father
was said to have a violent temper. His manners were those of
a well-bred man. He was as vigorous in his conduct as M. de
Salcedo was decrepit in his.

At the end of April, 1803, the *Argo*, a brig commanded by
Lieutenant Dusseuil, arrived from Dunkirk loaded with powder and war supplies. It had on board Captain Costille of the
artillery. The *Volcan*, an excellent gunboat also destined for
Louisiana, had run aground on the coast of England. The

Argo was ninety days in crossing and, in addition, took twenty days coming up from La Balise to this anchorage.

The United States had, by the treaty of 1793 [1795], obtained a right of deposit from His Catholic Majesty. Governor Salcedo suppressed it against the advice of the intendant, perhaps because of the spirit of rivalry and contradiction that existed between these two officials. The governor kept this controversy a secret from me. The intendant confided to me that he had had some bitter and unpleasant correspondence with M. de Salcedo about the affair. The Americans were highly incensed by this violation of a vested right. I expressed my astonishment to M. de Salcedo that, under the existing circumstances, he should raise such a question on his own authority and not have said anything to me about it. He replied that he had only meant to obey orders from his government, whose intention he thought he anticipated; but having made a report to the captain general in Havana, he would leave it at that as long as he had not received a decision from higher authorities.

Right of deposit

Our *chargé d'affaires* in Washington City, M. [Louis-André] Pichon, sent me an order from the court of Madrid, which reached me on May 17, insisting that its agents on the premises should leave things *in statu quo* until such time as Spain and the United States should come to a mutual understanding about another site for the right of deposit, if they so saw fit. So ended temporarily an affair about which the Americans had sought to create such a prodigious stir.

Another affair created no less a sensation in local circles. Captain Pierre Farnuel of the vessel *Africain*, which had left Bordeaux in July, 1802, notified me that he had been detained at Plaquemines. Coming from Senegal, he had, under the pretext of needing provisions, put into port at Havana. His real purpose, however, was to sell his cargo of slaves there, if he could not bring them to Louisiana. At Havana, [the merchant] Colson—sent by the Frenchman Roustan [Jacques Rouzan] as well as by the Louisianian [Jean-François] Mérieult [both of whom were also merchants] to Simon Poey,

The Roustan passes

a merchant from Havana—showed Poey some kind of passes from General [Claude] Victor, indeed from Job-Aimé [chief magistrate]. By these passes, the captain general [Victor], obviously urged on by the chief magistrate of Louisiana (and with the joint signatures of both), authorized the French flag to enter into this colony [Louisiana] and requested either Spanish or French commanders to allow the introduction of Negroes as well as other merchandise. The passes also contained an additional clause that they were valid for two weeks after arrival and not any longer. Simon Poey and Colson used one of these so-called passes to negotiate with Pierre Farnuel concerning his cargo, which would be payable in New Orleans at a price, in any case, greater on the average than 250 piastres fortes per head and by six-month drafts and other drafts payable in France.

Farnuel kept these arrangements from me and only told me that his ship had been fitted out by Placiart of Bordeaux. I wrote to the governor [Salcedo] requesting him to order Farnuel to come up the river as far as the city and be subject to examination of his papers upon arrival.

At one o'clock in the afternoon, Farnuel reappeared, informing me that Mérieult opposed his continuing, on the strength of an agreement that had been forced upon him in Havana under the pretense that he could enter New Orleans only if provided with passes from Captain General Victor. I told him that I had nothing whatsoever to do with it; but I could assure him that, loaded with merchandise under the French flag, he was welcome.

Mérieult and Roustan came running to me, showed me the passes from the captain general, and recriminated strongly against Farnuel's dishonesty. I pointed out that in all of this, the interest of the colony and the intentions of the French government had to be the sole motive for my conduct. These made it mandatory for me to facilitate the entrance of the slave ship into the harbor; but the rest was irrelevant to me. I pointed out, too, that above all, I knew nothing about passes from the captain general of Louisiana, issued in Paris for this region.

Portrait of Pierre Clément Laussat

Portrait of Madame Marie Anne Peborde Laussat

A view of the Laussat Papers, Journal, and *Mémoires*

Livre 1.

100 Exemplaires

Mémoires sur ma Vie,
à mon fils,
pendant les Années 1803 et suivantes,

~~dans le cours de~~ ~~publique~~ ~~jai rempli~~
~~que j'ai rempli des fonctions publiques, savoir :~~

à la Louisianne en qualité de Commissaire
du Gouvernement Français pour la reprise de
possession de cette Colonie et pour sa remise
aux États-Unis;

à la Martinique, comme Préfet Colonial;

à la Guyane Française, en qualité de
Commandant et administrateur, pour le Roi.

vixi et quem dederat cursum fortuna peregi.
Virgil. Æn. lib. 4.

par M. de Laussat (Pierre Clément)

1831.

200 pag. de mon écriture,
évaluées à environ
80 pag. in 8? de J. J. Rousseau
de Musset Pathey.

Courtesy of the Historic New Orleans Collection

The title page of Laussat's _Mémoires_ written in his own hand

The page from Laussat's *Mémoires* concerning the transfer of Louisiana to the United States on December 20, 1803

The certified copy appointing Laussat as colonial prefect of Louisiana. It is dated August 20, 1802, and signed by Admiral Denis Decrès, minister of the navy and colonies

Decree by Laussat establishing a municipal council for New Orleans
(November 30, 1803)

Bonaparte Premier Consul, au nom du Peuple Français, voulant activer l'exécution

Du Traité et des deux Conventions conclus et signés, le 10 floréal an 11, entre la République Française et les États-unis d'Amérique,
par le citoyen François Barbé-Marbois, Ministre du trésor public, et messieurs Robert R. Livingston et James Monroe,
Ministre plénipotentiaire des États-unis, tous trois munis de leurs pleins-pouvoirs, autorise le citoyen Pierre Clément Laussat à échanger
à recevoir les ratifications du dit Traité et des deux Conventions qui y sont jointes, et d'exécuter, à cet effet, les pouvoirs nécessaires Et comme l'objet
Du dit Traité est de faire passer aux États-unis la souveraineté et la propriété de la Colonie ou Province de la Louisiane, sous les mêmes clauses
à conditions qu'elle avait été cédée avant l'Espagne à la France, en vertu du Traité conclu à Saint Ildephonse, le neuf Vendémiaire, an neuf, entre
les deux derniers Louisianes, le Premier Consul, au nom du Peuple Français, donne au sieur Laussat, Préfet Colonial, plein et absolu
pouvoir, commission, et mandement spécial pour faire l'échange des ratifications du Traité et des Conventions du dix Floréal, an onze, à rendre, au nom de la République
Française, en qualité de Commissaire de son Gouvernement, aux Commissaires ou agents des États-unis dûment autorisés à cet effet, la possession, contrées et dépendances De
la Louisiane, conformément aux articles premier, second, quatre et cinq du Traité, lorsque lui-même aura reçu la dite Colonie des officiers de Sa Majesté
Catholique, en vertu des pouvoirs spéciaux qui lui sont remis par cet objet.

En foi de quoi, sont donnés les présentes, signées, contresignées, scellées du Sceau de la République.

À Saint-Cloud, le dix-sept Floréal, an onze de la République Française (Six-Cent-mil-huit cent-trois).

Le Ministre de la
Marine & des Colonies
Decrès

Par le Premier Consul
le Secrétaire d'État
H. Hugues Maret

PROCLAMATION.

AU NOM DE LA RÉPUBLIQUE FRANÇAISE.

PIERRE CLÉMENT LAUSSAT,

PRÉFET COLONIAL, COMMISSAIRE DU GOUVERNEMENT FRANÇAIS,

AUX LOUISIANAIS.

LOUISIANAIS,

La mission qui m'avait transporté à travers 2,500 lieues de mer, au milieu de vous, cette mission dans laquelle j'ai long-tems placé tant d'honorables espérances & tant de vœux pour votre bonheur, elle est aujourd'hui changée : celle dont je suis en ce moment le ministre & l'exécuteur, moins douce quoiqu'également flatteuse pour moi, m'offre une consolation, c'est qu'en général elle vous est encore beaucoup plus avantageuse.

En vertu des pouvoirs & des ordres respectifs, les Commissaires de S. M. C. viennent de me remettre le pays, & vous voyez les étendards flottans de la République Française & vous entendez le bruit répété de ses canons vous annoncer en ce jour de toutes parts le retour de sa domination sur ces Plages : elle n'y sera, LOUISIANAIS, que d'un instant, & je suis à la veille de les transmettre aux Commissaires

(2)

des États-Unis, chargés d'en prendre possession, au nom de leur Gouvernement Fédéral : ils sont près d'arriver ; je les attends.

Les approches d'une guerre commencée sous de sanglans & terribles auspices, & menaçant pour les quatre parties du monde, ont conduit le Gouvernement Français à reporter son attention & ses réflexions sur ces contrées : des vues de prudence & d'humanité, s'alliant à des vues d'une politique plus vaste, plus solide, dignes en un mot du génie qui balance à cette heure même de si grandes destinées parmi les Nations, ont alors donné une direction nouvelle aux intentions bienfaisantes de la France sur la Louisiane : elle l'a cédée aux États-Unis d'Amérique.

Vous devenez ainsi, LOUISIANAIS, le gage chéri d'une amitié qui ne peut manquer d'aller se fortifiant le jour en jour entre les deux Républiques & qui doit contribuer si puissamment à leur commun repos & à leur commune prospérité.

L'article III du Traité ne vous échappera point :
" Les Habitans, y est-il dit, des territoires cédés se-
" ront incorporés dans l'union des États-Unis, &
" admis, aussitôt qu'il sera possible, d'après les prin-
" cipes de la Constitution Fédérale, à la jouissance
" de tous les droits, avantages & immunités, des Ci-
" toyens des États-Unis, &, en attendant, ils feront
" maintenus & protégés dans la jouissance de leurs
" liberté, propriétés & dans l'exercice des religions
" qu'ils professent ".

Public proclamation by Laussat announcing the official possession of Louisiana by France and discussing the transfer of the colony to the United States and the resulting benefits to the inhabitants

Portrait of
William Augustus Bowles

Entering Louisiana at the Balize, or the mouth of the Mississippi River,
as painted in 1834 by J. H. B. Latrobe

Roustan then changed his mind and called them, not passes, but letters of recommendation. He did not so much as open his mouth about those from Job-Aimé, with which he was likewise provided. I let him talk on. I summed up what I had said by pointing out that he was badly mistaken if he claimed that the French flag could not be admitted into Louisiana on the same terms as the Spanish, or that African Negroes could not be admitted on the strength of our laws and my authorization. As for all the rest, I washed my hands of the matter.

Noticing a certain hesitancy on the part of the governor and some partiality in favor of Mérieult and Roustan, I opposed him on the general principle that Negro slaves coming directly from Africa could be introduced freely, and pointed out that we, as administrators, ought to be above such underhanded scheming and mercantile chicanery. I demanded a prompt permission for Captain Farnuel.

About ten days had elapsed when Roustan and Mérieult brought legal proceedings against Farnuel before the Spanish auditor. Three 1-hour interrogations took place; the names of the captain general and the commissioner of justice, and rumors about their passes, etc., were tossed around. The whole town gossiped wantonly. These proceedings seemed to me scandalous and improper, apt to discredit beforehand the French officials and to compromise the dignity of their government. Not content with jeopardizing his own name, the chief magistrate had evidently tricked the captain general. I sent for Roustan and Mérieult, Captain Farnuel, and his consignee, Saint-Marc. After a lengthy conference, I let them know that I expected this whole business to be settled and ended without a trace. Receiving no overture for conciliation from either party, I enjoined them to choose two arbitrators each to judge without appeal—either by legal procedure or by amicable agreement, whichever way would be satisfactory. These arbitrators should themselves choose a fifth person with whom they would pronounce judgment. They were to submit the names of their choice to me within twenty-four hours.

The following day Mérieult and Roustan brought in the names of Messrs. Labatut and Soulier; and for Farnuel and Saint-Marc, those of Messrs. Lanusse and Faurie. Along with these names, they handed to me their signatures affixed to a blank page, and I sent it to the respective arbitrators that very same evening.

Nevertheless, Farnuel had received a summons from the persistent auditor and, foreseeing that the Spanish judge was going to confiscate the two so-called passes, he took care to leave them in my hands; I passed them on to the arbitrators, making it clear to them that once their verdict concluded the argument, these documents should be returned to Roustan and should disappear. I have heard no more talk of it, and malicious Spaniards and Americans were deprived of food for gossip, with which they had hoped to amuse themselves at our expense.

While we waited for the French expedition to arrive, our days rolled along quite monotonously. Word reached me that a prolonged icy winter had delayed its departure from Helvoët-Sluys. Generally, we used to retire at about ten o'clock, sometimes at nine, to screen ourselves against the mosquitoes, which, at sunset, swarm down from the horizon into every nook and cranny of the apartments. They flit forth about the lights and sharply deliver a sting with their darts, covering the arms and hands with smarting bumps that become infected upon the slightest touch. It is impossible either to read or to write; even the living room, despite the diversion of many people's presence, becomes a torture chamber. Only a passion for cards and a body toughened by habit can render such discomfort endurable.

Our lodgings at the gates of the city, some thirty paces from the ramparts, were still regarded as being beyond the city limits. The sun or the rain, the dust or the mud were often obstacles [for visitors]. Some people came in a carriage. But not all had one, and for those who did, its use was pretentious for so short a distance. As a result, except for formal receptions, few people called, especially after eight or nine o'clock in the evening. We appreciated no less the advantage of being in a comfortable house in charming surroundings, with fresh, cool air, if it was cool anywhere. Whenever we returned home, we felt renewed pleasure at being there again. My library was my delight. I had there, within my reach, my precious collection of books and my favorite authors.[41]

In the last days of May, we received the first rumors of a disagreement between London and Paris. England was making extensive preparations. The British ambassador had some heated exchanges with the First Consul during an audience. Official accounts had been submitted to the Parliament in London and to the Corps Législatif in Paris. Discussions were ominous. These rumors, which seemed more or less serious according to one's disposition, did not make my position here any easier. I took the stand of isolation and silence.

May 30

The American General, [Jonathan] Dayton of New Jersey, had, in 1787, at the age of twenty-six, signed the Constitution of the United States. A former member of the American Convention, a present member of the Senate, of which he was also president (speaker) more than once, he was in New Orleans at that time. He was accompanied by Dearborn, the eighteen-year-old son of the secretary of war. The two travelers had met in the Ohio Territory with Escher, the clever and talented Swiss confidential secretary of the firm of Hottinger and Company of Paris. General Dayton was tall and spare, with a cold, reserved bearing. We dined together at the Spanish governor's house and at mine. He looked for an occasion to speak with me. He admitted that he had undertaken this trip to become acquainted with a region of great interest to the United States and about which there was much talk in both houses of Congress, without any real knowledge. He did not conceal the reasons why they regarded with anxiety the possibility of the French becoming its possessors:

1. They dreaded the ambitious prospects and the enterprising nature of the nation.
2. They could not help fearing that crowd of restless men who have nothing to lose; who bring with them a rugged and adventurous spirit (I am translating his own words here); whom our

country would foist upon this colony to get rid of them; and who, in one way or another, would come to blows with their neighbors.

3. They saw with distress the two powers becoming neighbors in a thousand places, thus giving frequent causes for disputes when until then there had been only reasons for living in peace.

4. Last, they were especially suspicious that we might want to foment divisive wars between their western and eastern states; arouse separatist ideas among the states; stir up the Indians; and kindle underhandedly enmities and troubles against their government.

To the first [of these reasons], I explained the policy of France when she desired to recover Louisiana: This policy was to have a region in which to settle her excess population—in other words, to have a part of America where interest toward France could be cultivated, just as the maritime countries of Europe have found it convenient to do, though foreseeing the future independence of the whole of America.

To the second, we would introduce four types of men: Black slaves, whom it was my principle to approve only temporarily and with moderation in lower Louisiana only;[42] hired troops, who would be stationed here in limited numbers only, and who would be among the best and most disciplined military men in the world; farmers, who would be from established families, chosen from among the hardest-working people in the world; and, finally, those restless and passionate men of whom it would be advantageous for the Republic to rid itself on the Continent. But they would be carefully confined to the interior, far from the river and away from contact with other people, together with vigilant and strict administrative supervision.

To the third, France would have, on the contrary, more reason than ever to be considerate of the United States government. It is essentially not maritime and colonial or commercial and seafaring, like England. I developed the idea in accordance with this comparison and tried to point out that we would be, for the United States, western neighbors they could mistrust less than they did the English in the northeast and the north.

To the fourth: "This objection," I said, "has been harped upon in your discussions, your pamphlets, and your newspapers, which proves that, to borrow a concise and proverbial expression, 'you feel where the shoe pinches.' Is it our fault if the ties between your states in the East and your states in the West are unnatural? All I can reply is that, should your western states secede and join Louisiana, the ties of Louisiana itself to France would obviously be weakened. It is not, therefore, in our interest to provoke it. What is more, our mission is to nurture unceasingly the best possible understanding between ourselves and the United States government."

I have submitted the gist of our conference and how I *June* played my role in it. Deep down in my heart, I admitted that General Dayton was right. Undoubtedly, under present conditions and as long as the European peoples keep the present system of colonization, I firmly maintain that France should resume her former domination over Louisiana. In her hands, it should soon become the finest of colonies; but it would undoubtedly be more advantageous for her in most respects, and no less so for the United States, that it become part of their confederation. Then it would develop its full potential and rank among the richest countries on the globe.

By the same Ohio route which brought these travelers, *Ships* there arrived a schooner and a frigate, built by M. Berthoud, *brought* a Swiss, of Pittsburgh, formerly Fort Duquesne. It took *down from* forty-eight days to float down the Ohio and Mississippi, in- *Pittsburgh* cluding sixteen days of layover along the way. The rapids down the Ohio were thirteen to fourteen English feet deep. The two vessels hadn't run as much risk there as on the Mississippi, where it was often impossible to steer; yet the current swept over uprooted trees, around which the vessels had to steer. In any case, these two vessels reached this port safe and sound. The Allegheny mountains, eight hundred leagues inland, offered them as a gift to the sea! They will have traveled sixteen hundred leagues to get back there, although it is only one hundred leagues from the one place to the other by land. But that road is terrible.

Pittsburgh had no more than two thousand souls but was

growing daily. Situated at the upper entrance to Kentucky, it witnessed countless migrations from the New England states through this gateway. Each winter saw a continuous trek of hundreds of families passing through, transferring their residences beyond the mountains. Kentucky, Tennessee, Ohio, and Indiana have already been born of it; still others will be. The French people would like to be able to follow this example, having regions to spread into. One should see with what enthusiasm they poured into Louisiana when it had just been opened to them. Merchant vessels from Marseilles, from Bordeaux, and from Le Havre kept coming in, every one with fifteen or twenty passengers on board.

June 19   Rumors of the cession to the United States were gaining ground as I realized easily. The fluctuations of the political thermometer in this respect were indicated by the greater or lesser eagerness with which people sought me—and that eagerness was on the decline.

M. Bowls   For the moment, however, an incident distracted public attention. Bowls [William Augustus Bowles] was brought by an escort of Indians to the Spanish prison of this city. Born in Maryland, he was, before the [American] Revolution, an officer in an English regiment at a military post in Pensacola shortly before the Spaniards, under Galvés, took over. He was dismissed from his regiment for misconduct. It is said that he went to New York, where he joined some adventurers and actors, and went on to Providence [New Providence Island in the British West Indies]. Lord Dunmore was governor of the Bahama Islands. William Ponton [Panton], an English merchant from Pensacola, was doing a thriving business in furs. He had sent [to the Bahamas] his associate [John] Forbes, who had some financial dispute with the governor. Lord Dunmore was censured in·London. In order to revenge himself, he determined to seize the lucrative fur trade in the Floridas from the Ponton firm. By agreement with Miller, a rich settler in Providence who was acting as an agent for the governor, he chose Bowls to go settle among the Indians and to build up trade there at the expense of Ponton.

Bowls went among the Seminoles, or Creoles [Laussat is

wrong here; he really means the southern Creek Indians],
along the Apalachicola River. There he met with some difficulties and returned to Providence with five Indians. Lord
Dunmore shipped him off to Quebec; from Quebec he was
sent to London, always taking along his five Indians. The
English government received them cordially [Bowls was recognized as the ambassador from the Indian nations], hoping
thereby to win the goodwill of the Indian nations. They
started out again, with a few gifts of good or inferior
weapons, and returned to Providence on a ship belonging to
Miller. There the governor gave him twenty fellow soldiers of
fortune and sent them back into the Floridas.

Upon their arrival they joined cause with some Seminoles,
who helped them seize Ponton's storehouses at Saint-Marc-
des-Apalaches. This was an act of aggression against the
Spaniards because Spain had sold Ponton the exclusive
privilege of the fur trade there. Therefore, Baron de Carondelet, the governor of Louisiana and Florida, took action in
this matter. He sent a small expedition composed of [Jóse
Bernardo de] Hévia, today commander of the port at New
Orleans; [Pierre-Georges] Rousseau, a naval officer who had
obtained promotion by his own merit, and a settler in the
colony; and a few other officers to seize the adventurer
Bowls. They were sent to the commandant of the fort at
Apalaches. The latter thought it best to draw Bowls to his
house under some pretext, but agreed to do so only if they
gave their word of honor they would not do violence to the
person of Bowls. But once he was there, neither commander
of the fort nor Hévia bothered any longer about the promise.
Rousseau insisted on keeping his word, but they did not
listen to him. Bowls was seized, put on board a vessel, taken
to New Orleans, sent to Havana, then to Spain, and from
Spain to the Philippines. There his presence frightened the
aging governor, who could already imagine him inciting the
Indians in his country. He shipped him back to Europe.

The vessel carrying Bowls sailed in convoy from the Ile de
France [Mauritius, an island in the Indian Ocean] in ships which
Messrs. de Sercey and Mahon, our naval officers, were taking

back to Europe. Bowls tried more than once during the crossing to plot against the captain of the ship but failed each
time. Finally, during a layover on the coast of Africa, in
Senegal if I am not mistaken, he escaped—aided, they say,
by some Frenchmen. First he reached Jamaica, then London,
then Providence, and the Floridas. There he announced his
arrival by a raid on the fort at Apalaches, which he took. For
having capitulated, the commander was tried by court-
martial, which went on for two years. During that time the
commander was kept in prison. Yet Bowls did not stop crossing swords with the Ponton firm, or rather with Forbes, since
Ponton had died.

Bowls was most active among the Indians, where he en-
hanced his influence and offset that of the Anglo-Americans,
who feared and detested him as did the Spaniards. The
Anglo-Americans claimed that he had sent pirate expeditions
to sea and given them letters of marque. Not long ago, in May
of last year, the Creoles [Creek Indians] held an assembly of
their confederation. He wanted to attend either to further the
interests of his adopted nation, the Seminoles [a tribe within
the Creek Confederacy], or in order to confound thereby the
intrigues of Anglo-Americans and of the Forbes party.

The usual place for such assemblies was considered sacred
and no one bore arms there. Bowls was accompanied by a
chief and another Indian. He had refused to let three hundred
of his warriors come with him. Someone invited him to go
have a drink of milk in one of the huts. While he was inside,
fifteen Indians pounced upon him unexpectedly. Forbes was
twenty paces off, visibly pale and shamefaced. They seized
Bowls, dragged him by force for half a league, threw him into
a canoe, and took off for Mobile. His abductors having fallen
asleep, he plunged into the water and swam ashore; his Indian guards dashed after him, and tracked him down again.

At Mobile, Bowls was turned over to M. [Joaquim] Ossorne, the Spanish commander, son-in-law of Madame [Gil-
bert] Maxent of New Orleans. Ossorne brought him to the city
escorted by five Indians, among whom was the chief who had
agreed to betray him for four thousand piastres fortes, half

payable by the Spanish government, and half by the Forbes company. After two or three days, on Tuesday, June 14, Bowls was put on board a schooner; and Governor Salcedo's son, his warden, conducted him to Havana. Bowls exhibited courage and composure. The manner in which he had been apprehended and his other personal adventures created public interest in him. He would eventually die in a prison cell.

The Indians who had brought him wished to see me and were introduced to me on Monday, June 13, 1803, by Fabre, the Spanish interpreter, and M. Devilliers. Chief Tastiki of the Topalca, a man about fifty-five years old, was an "esteemed one"; another "esteemed one" who spoke Choctaw acted as intermediary for the chief and our interpreter Fabre; a third "esteemed one" was a half-breed Englishman. With them also were the chief's son and one of his friends, both of them fifteen years old.[43] All had a proud and confident air, an agile and graceful carriage, a handsome stature, and faces showing strength of character. The chief seemed to command imperiously. He rose, pressed me to his bosom, and shaking my hand, assured me that he remembered having known the French in his youth and that he had always hoped to see them again.

After a few vague speeches, I proposed refreshments. They accepted, "in order to drink a toast to the chief of the French," they added. Tastiki, glass in hand, expressed himself something like this: "I have often thought that a huge cloud covered our horizon, but that a wind blowing from the other side of the great lake would arise and disperse it." We clinked glasses.

I am not going to say anything about their dress, which was just as it has been described a hundred times. The chief before me was reputed to be quite an unprincipled rogue. In his day, he had committed many atrocities. Once he had entered a plantation where he killed everybody and pillaged it. It was said that Bowls once commented with some bitterness, "There is nothing worse than half-civilized Indians." Governor Salcedo, speaking to Tastiki, expressed surprise at his boldness to have dared to kidnap Bowls right in the midst of

Visit by the Indians

the Creole [Creek Indian] assembly. "Sir," he retorted, "you gave me four thousand piastres for that; if someone gave me six thousand for kidnapping you from this city in front of your own garrison, I would do it."

The Mississippi, which flowed beneath my windows, presented a new spectacle each day and never ceased to interest me. *Meschacebé* or *Michacépi*—which in the language of the Indians means "Old Man Far Off"—is not difficult to control despite its enormous volume and its course of twelve hundred to fifteen hundred leagues. Its floods in lower Louisiana are neither extensive nor dangerous. The two tongues of land across which it flows from the beginning of its delta at Pointe-Coupée, slope gently downward from their banks to the lakes and bayous on the right and the left, which flow out into the sea. In this manner, a stream of water escaping from the river through its banks, if directed into a little canal, will form a flowing stream and, growing larger, form a small gully, then a rivulet, and then a river, whereby it empties rapidly into the lakes.

From the disposition of land and water, there resulted a great facility for setting up mills when the river is high. Here, as in Egypt, they say that "the flood is good or bad." The last one was quite good. The seasonal low is always announced by storms. We had one every day, often evening and morning, beginning on the ninth of May and lasting to October. By the end of June, the water level was up four feet. Some occasional floods, which no longer followed the invariable rise and fall of the river, still occured unexpectedly.

River banks that I never knew before came into view right under my eye. The river flowed majestically and peacefully in its bed, whose banks rose abruptly here, sloped gently there. I caught sight of exposed *écores* [high river banks] and battures [exposed soil deposited along the inner shore by action of the current]. We saw this beautiful river from our living room, spreading out like a circular sheet of water ruffled gently by a wind from the north; its changing reflection varied with the color of the sky. Trees obstructed its course. Far out could be seen immense stretches of typical Dutch meadows with tall cypress trees staked off like a rampart. Innumerable herds of oxen, cows, horses, and sheep roamed there all day long. The mooring at the minimum depth of the river was still more than thirty fathoms. At the solstices, the sun set at seven o'clock.

The great heat waves began about mid-June with stifling mornings, a storm in the afternoon, and in the evening a coolness that was deeply appreciated. It was said that the summer of 1803 was less unbearable than usual. During the month of August we even had some dismal days interspersed with fresh air. The sun alone was scorching; its rays darted forth ruthlessly upon the body. The thermometer, in the shade of my study, registered as high as thirty-two degrees; its average was twenty-eight or twenty-nine [about 84° F.]. Some days were unbearable—like the desert heat of Africa, as I imagine it. One no longer heard the warbling of birds; one scarcely saw any of them flitting about. July especially moved along as if escorted by Sirius with his flaming breath. A breeze from the north in mid-September announced cooler weather. It was preceded by a deluge of rains without strong wind or storm. The water poured down from all corners of the heavens like so many swollen springs, and dispersed swiftly in torrents in all directions. The surplus moisture in the atmosphere covered my books with a permanent mildew. A pair of boots hung up in a clean place became green with mildew within three or four days at most. This quality of dampness in the air must not be harmful. People have good complexions; and septuagenarians, octogenarians, and nonagenarians are less rare than in most parts of Europe.

Yellow fever comes during the season known as "dog days." Here it is especially known for the ravages it causes among foreigners in general and among numerous farmers from the western states, who come here just about that time to sell their commodities. I had an attack of it on the first of July. I had brought along from Paris to New Orleans a person with an inquiring mind, who was a naturalist and a savant—Dr. Blanquet Ducaila, professor of chemistry, whom M. Chaptal had recommended to me. I declared from the very first day of my illness that I wanted no other doctor. He justified my confidence, but nature saved me by provoking a severe noseblood that occurred on the third day of my fever and left me more dead than alive for several hours. The entire city, even the doctors, hastened to congratulate my wife about it—I was really out of danger. However, the climate and spells of excessive heat retarded and prolonged my convalescence. I was laid up for twenty-five days and did not feel my natural self once more until after four months.[44] While I lay on my sick bed, we received official confirmation that war had been declared between France and England [May 18, 1803]. My situation was not improved with that news.

M. L'Adjutant Burthe   At the same time, the conduct of Adjutant [André] Burthe spread trouble, as I must relate, however reluctantly. Burthe had become a second lieutenant of the dragoons at the beginning of the Revolution, after studying under the direction of a parish priest in Lorraine. His father, an ex-soldier, joined some manufacturing enterprise in Metz. The son, in turn, took up the cause of the Revolution with a passion. He entered the general staff as an adjutant through the endorsement of M. Solignac, then adjutant general and later lieutenant general. The adjutant became aide-de-camp to General Masséna. During a sortie at the siege of Genoa, Burthe was wounded by a musket ball. The general raised him to the rank of adjutant general, a promotion confirmed on July 14, 1800. Named chief of staff of the troops in Holland commanded by General Victor, he followed him with the same rank in the Louisiana expedition.[45]

He knew my neighbor in Paris, M. Sillan, who had spoken to me of him in glowing terms and had arranged a meeting between us. I soon had occasion to be convinced that, judging from his tone and demeanor, he felt himself highly qualified because of his experience in the military. General Victor commissioned him to go with me ahead of the Louisiana expedition. Burthe blurted out one day, regarding this assignment, that he would take charge of the personnel of the troops and I of the supplies and equipment. "No!" I replied to him. "You will not take charge of anything except under my orders." These words offended him. He sought to antagonize General Victor against me, which resulted in explanations between the general and myself. The First Consul and the minister did not support claims contrary to my prerogatives. The plan to have Burthe leave with me fell through and Major Vinache took his place.

At the farewell dinner given by the minister of the navy, I told General Victor that I would be annoyed if what had happened had provoked him and changed his mind about giving me Burthe as a travel companion. He seized upon the proposal. The next morning, Burthe was at my house, informing me that he would join me at Rochefort. He arrived there without orders from the minister, without a passport, and without permission to come on board ship. I had to intervene with the naval prefect, write to Paris, and put myself to a good deal of trouble in order to remove the difficulties that detained him. In reply, the minister sent orders to Admiral Martin [naval prefect at Rochefort] to take Burthe aboard the *Surveillant* or the *Citoyen* or any other vessel sailing for Louisiana.

We boarded our ship. The opinion that I had formed of this officer was soon confirmed. Conceit and irascibility were his two predominant faults. He did not, however, lack intelligence, but he had a disorderly mind. He was essentially imbued with revolutionary ideas. All that he understood, that he professed, and that he loved about French liberty was military despotism. On board ship, he gave vent to these sentiments without any restraint. As a consequence there arose some rather noisy squabbles. He boasted of not having subscribed to the plebiscite appointing the First Consul for life [1802] and not believing in Jacobins.

He avoided my presenting him to Admiral Martin, the naval prefect at Rochefort, and had been careful never to accompany me on visits to the Spanish commander. He made his visits apart and presented his letters from General Victor, pretending to have a separate role [in Louisiana].

He went to inspect the barracks, hospitals, and so on, and made out requisitions without my knowledge. I disdained to take any notice of his immature and inconsequential conduct. He forced me, however, on certain occasions to point out to him categorically that I could only respect his rank here socially and out of propriety; that he was in Louisiana without orders; and that there was no French representative or chief here other than myself, whereupon he asked me whether I had acknowledged the orders coming from the captain general. "I have," I replied, "the utmost consideration for the wishes of the captain general; as for an order, none such exists from him to me, and I only know of the orders of the First Consul and of the minister."

Two days later (May 12, 1803), we were invited to a dinner given by the governor to honor the Marquis de Casacalvo and myself. He did not appear and used a thousand intrigues to prevent Vinache, chief of engineers, who was expressly assigned to me, from going. He did not respond to my invitation to the dinner I gave the following Sunday. I ceased paying any attention to him at all.

June 3 When the news of the cession was widely circulated, Burthe called on me in full dress uniform to assure me that circumstances obliged him to reconcile himself with me. True, his prospects for marrying Mlle Dulaur [Delord Sarpy] could well have contributed to his taking this step. Be that as it may, I had learned well from his past conduct what stand was most judicious to take with him, and, while perfectly polite, I always maintained this line of behavior toward him.

He affected haughty airs and an extremely imperious tone before people and in the presence of his inferiors. He used it before M. Vinache, who, he thought, seemed susceptible enough to be impressed by it, and in the presence of M. Costille, captain of artillery, who made fun of it. July 14, the day on which I usually hosted officials at dinner, was drawing close. He took the initiative and invited these two guests. M. Vinache accepted only conditionally. M. Burthe flew to him, found Vinache in his yard, refused to enter his apartment, and took him to task. Cursing and swearing like a fishwife, Burthe declared that there was only one chief here—himself—and that to teach him this, he would place

Vinache under arrest. Vinache answered that he recognized
no other chief but me and that, to teach him that, he would
not consider himself being under arrest. Burthe left in a rage
and issued his arrest by a letter in which he assured him that
he would be obeyed at any cost—if necessary, by force!
Vinache passed these documents on to me, and I wrote to
Burthe. I reminded him in restrained terms of the limits of his
powers. He answered me with an incredible, inconceivable
insolence—belittling, insulting, defying, and threatening me.

I sent word to the governor and the Marquis de Casacalvo
requesting them to please come to my house, where my con-
valescing condition kept me confined. I explained what had
occurred. I made it clear to them that the First Consul would
not pardon me if I did not stand firm, that I was going to issue
warrants for the arrest of this officer and for his return to
France, and that I expected them to facilitate the carrying out
of this order.

We agreed on the matter. Consequently, the very next day,
I sent them my decree. They kept it three days, after which
time they responded, suggesting that I substitute more lenient, equivalent measures, such as forbidding Burthe and
Vinache to trespass certain limits. Burthe merely promised to
discontinue his repeated offenses against Vinache and to depart at once for France. On my part, I insisted upon the
execution pure and simple of my order. I did not obtain it,
whereupon I submitted an account of the matter to the minister.

On the following October 14, I was invited to a dinner
given by the Marquis de Casacalvo on the occasion of the
name day of the Prince of Asturias. I attended. As I was
stepping out of my carriage, I was informed that Burthe's
cabriolet and liveryman were at the door. I went on in. A few
minutes elapsed. I noticed Burthe dressed in his uniform and
I stopped short: "Since Burthe is here," I said at once, "I am
no longer." "But why, M. le Préfet?" exclaimed the marquis. I proceeded to leave and he accompanied me. "Burthe,"
I continued, "may no longer appear by my side as a French
officer. I am very sorry." I listened to no more. I bade good-

day to the company, and my attendants followed me. I got back into my carriage.

If I had accidentally met Burthe anywhere else, I would have taken no notice of the incident. But invited as a representative of the French government, after what had transpired between the governor, the marquis, and myself concerning Burthe, I could not have conducted myself otherwise with dignity.[46] The following week, Burthe asked me, through the intermediary of the Spanish governor, to pay him his salary. I refused on the grounds that anything relating to this officer depended hereafter on the First Consul and was exclusively within his jurisdiction.

He presented a pitiful spectacle in Louisiana during the operations for the retrocession by the Spaniards till the transfer to the United States. He complained far and wide of not playing the role which he claimed. He had himself alone to blame if I did not give him the foremost rank after my own.[47] Owing to his *savoir-faire*, his stay in Louisiana improved his fortune. A widow, Madame Dulaur, lived half a league from town with two interesting daughters. She was wealthy. He maneuvered so cleverly that not only did he marry the older daughter, who had a dowry of sixteen thousand piastres fortes, but in addition, he married off the younger daughter to a young man bearing his name [Dominique Burthe], his nephew. At the death of their mother, they would inherit more than 400,000 francs each.

The happy couple finally booked passage secretly for New York with Captain Jackwais of the American brig *Pastley*, which they went to meet on January 18 [1804], several leagues downriver. On departing, the bridegroom bequeathed to me clandestinely a touching souvenir entitled *Burthe contre Laussat*, with the epigraph, "Facit indignatio versum" [Juvenal, *Satire*: "Indignation makes the verse"]. He distributed this publication secretly. Its principal merit was a perfidious misinterpretation of my conduct, tending to represent me as an enemy of the French army and of its greatest generals. This pamphlet was intended for France, where he hoped for some powerful results. In it he traced clearly his plan of attack from

the very moment of his arrival. I picked out twenty-two fal-
lacies in the first five pages and then stopped. It was beneath
me to respond. Besides, my conduct had the full approbation
of the government.

Among my associates, Burthe had not spared M. [Jean-
Paul] Blanque, commissioner of war, who had served in the
same army. I could never prevail upon Blanque to disregard
this attack. He avenged himself bitterly. I had not yet left
Louisiana, when on the eleventh of April "The Reply of Blanque to Burthe" was published. The latter had no need of
these scathing lines.

Still, I often reflected with regret how unfortunate had
been this fracas, which several times involved most unpleas-
antly the temporary representatives of France in Louisiana.
In my eagerness to dismiss this episode, I have related everything up to Burthe's departure and, consequently, up to the
spring of 1804, without considering whether I was anticipating
him by several months. I wanted, above all, to avoid having
to return to the subject. But I again take up a chronological
account.

The awaiting of the final outcome seemed to break the ties
of interest that had grown daily between Louisianians and
myself and already to isolate me noticeably from the inhabitants. I wondered what we would have in common before too
long. For whom did my opinions, my reflections still matter? Who, on seeing me, would think, "Our prosperity, our
wealth, our good fortune are very much in his hands"?
What settler would bother if I employed my time well or
badly?

I had really believed that I would always employ my time
usefully in this country, and I did not count on long periods
of leisure. And yet, there were periods of idleness despite my
impatience. So as not to waste that time and to derive, at least,
some benefit from it, I jotted down general notions and
memories that would one day describe the colony and recall
in detail the state in which I found it; and these I will compile
now. Unable to pride myself on what I would have done with
the colony, I will at least relate what I observed there.

July,
1803

I spent the remaining days of the month of July slowly nursing myself to complete recovery, swallowing *quinquina* [quinine solution] and hoping for the return of my strength. My door was closed; my health demanded it and, besides, it was sort of a duty. It would not do to officiate as a representative when war made my existence here precarious and my rank questionable. It would not have been proper for me to jeopardize anyone's chances with another government, which I might offend, as long as that individual was not assured that a change of government would not work to his detriment.[48]

July
and
August

Our daily routine was monotonous enough.[49] We spoke frequently of France. In our anxiety to receive news for which we were impatient, we exhausted our imagination conjecturing ways and means to hasten its arrival. My convalescence came to an end. The hours passed, all alike. We arose at six, had breakfast at seven, and lunched between two and three. After dinner, we took a walk around the galleries to chat for a while and receive visitors. We retired regularly at ten o'clock, but not before we cursed hundreds of times the swarms of gnats and mosquitoes which devoured us.

The few foreigners who visited us protested vehemently against the cession made by France. Together we talked over our troubles on these distant shores and the joy of returning to France. I resumed my weekly informal dinners at which I rallied the Frenchmen, whom our expedition had thrown into my orbit.

Difficulties
of animal
life during
the winter
or in the
summer
heat

The difficulties one encountered during the summer in procuring the necessities of life were hardly in keeping with the wealth and civilization of the city. Provisions were lacking in the market and were had only at prohibitive prices. Aside from the fact that the settler fluctuated in his speculations and in his tillage, and that he passed expeditiously from one endeavor to another, the growth in population, the affluence of the foreigners, and the progress of luxury at this moment were such that it will take some time before the supply equals demand. We imitated the colonists. Almost like farmers ourselves, we drew as they did upon our own resources, and our poultry yard came alive with hens, roosters, chicks, fatted pullets, turkeys (both domesticated ones raised in our aviary or wild ones hunted in the woods), domestic and wild geese, peacocks, bustards, ducks, sheep, deer, and raccoons. We set up a useful menagerie that was prolific, made a pretty sight, and provided amusement below our galleries.

At the time of our arrival, the meat in the markets was bad. Winter freezes the grass and Louisianians do not harvest hay. The food was not at all palatable from February to July, the season when the cattle fatten and become excellent. Sheep from the individual farmer was fat and good, but that from the butcher was lean and tasteless. They slaughtered the calves too late; the meat was no longer edible. The poultry came in quantity from Terre aux Boeufs and, when purchased in the marketplace, was disgusting. The *papabots*, a kind of plover, and the *grasset*, of the species of warblers, were a fat and delicate wild game. The partridges, which looked more like our quail than our partridges, were abundant and made good eating.

Havana sent us sea turtles, some of which I kept alive for a long time in a tub of fresh water. The Mississippi furnished the soft-shell turtle (*testudo ferox*) which connoisseurs prefer. It is irascible and mean and has a head like a serpent. From under its carapace a long, pointed snout and a pair of beady eyes project. It lifts its head boldly. Cooks in these regions prepare these animals perfectly.

Among the fish, the redfish, the eel, and the sea perch especially are greatly prized. The vegetables were not nearly so substantial and succulent as those of France. The peach, fig, plum, apple, and grape were introduced early into the colony. The peach is the fruit which grows best here. We received some as gifts on numerous occasions. The grapes were small, red, and sour. They were indigenous to this part of America. The best fruit of the country is without question the orange. Orange groves and that whole family of trees and shrubs multiplied there on all sides and were of the best grade. The pecan was similar to our nuts and was better.[50]

The colonist enjoyed numerous noisy festivities: eating,

June, July, August, and September

June 5

having a drinking glass in hand, harmonizing in song, and spending whole nights at frenzied card games. It was in the country that one really gave vent to these orgies. The Louisianian cannot resist friendliness and affability, but any semblance of arrogance or pride arouses him. I had no official excuse for resisting these invitations. So I yielded and accepted the one sent by M. Bronier, commander of the mounted troops of the militia and a wealthy planter living half a league downriver. The Spanish chiefs and many military officers were present. A thick dome of foliage on the lawn shaded a table set for approximately fifty persons. Just as they were being seated, a snake fell from the trees and was promptly killed.

This territory teems with snakes. My daughters had not been here more than a week when, upon descending the steps of our house one day, they stopped, struck with wonder. We rushed up. An orange-red snake whose sting is deadly slithered just two feet away from them. One day someone brought into our living room a live rattlesnake tied firmly by the head with a strong cord. It was wild. You may be sure that we all kept our distance. At the sight of us, it coiled up; then lifting itself up on its tail and darting its forked tongue, it sprang at us, its beady eyes flashing. Its very presence there, its sinuous movements, tied firmly though it was, terrified us, and I ordered it to be taken away at once. It lived six more weeks in a cask without eating. One day, a sailor boy about eleven or twelve years old was left to watch the house. Since he saw it with its eyes closed and motionless, he approached and touched it. The animal rattled its tail, became angry, and bit the child, who died. They killed the snake, but too late. It was quite easy to kill: a blow on its back or on its head with a stick or even a rod will do it. The rattlesnake is the king of these reptiles. It is the most generous of them, attacking or biting only when menaced or in danger. We know that its rattle is produced by the vibration of the jointed scales which strike against each other at the end of its tail. The Louisianians claim that it charms quadrupeds, birds, frogs, etc., which it wants to make its prey. I heard this from eyewitnesses whose word is credible.

Professional hunters frequently come upon snakes, especially rattlesnakes. At first they are frightened. They mentioned still another reptile frequently found in the deep swamps of the Atakapas, which is even more dangerous than the rattlesnake because, without having to coil up or make any sound, it darts up unexpectedly to the height of six or even eight feet and bites you with its volatile and instant poison. The country is so infested with snakes that one day, in my poultry yard, my cook, having picked up a setting turkey, found his bare arm immediately entwined by a large puff adder that was eating the eggs. The poor man got off with a good scare. After this digression regarding snakes, I will resume the story of my visits in the country.

I had not gone back to the plantation of Madame Siben since the time she gave a splendid dinner in my honor when I first arrived in the colony. I made my entrance into New Orleans from there. I went to thank her in mid-August. Madame Siben was the sister of Madame de Livaudais. Downstream from the city there were thirty-four plantations between my house and hers, all belonging to distinguished families. I took great pleasure in observing them. *July, August, September, October, and November*

Going back up the river, I invited myself to dinner at M. Boré's. I had refused invitations to his formal dinners, and I surprised him at home with his family. He gave me a tour of his properties, his gardens, his walks lined with trees, his sugarcane fields, and his establishments. His last sugar crop (1802) had been about eighty thousand pounds of sugar, which was considered of premium quality in lower Louisiana.

M. de Mira [Don Estevan Rodriques Miró, governor from 1785 to 1791] received some *islèges* [*islènes*] (Canarians) sent by Spain in 1783. They brought plantings of sugarcane which they had picked up in Havana on the way. They were peasants given to small farm cultivation. Soliés [Manuel Solis], one of their number, observed that war had priced *tafia* [a crude whiskey extract made from sugarcane] prohibitively in

New Orleans, and he used the product of his cane to manufacture some, which he sold for fifty to sixty piastres fortes. But in peacetime, his manufacturing fell off.

Discouraged by the loss of his indigo, M. Boré, in spite of the prejudices of Louisianians and the entreaties of his family, substituted sugarcane. He took up a partnership with [Antoine] Morin, a refiner. Success did not prevent them from having disagreements, and the following year they broke up their partnership. Morin, however, claimed the honor of having introduced the growing of sugarcane into this country.[51] After that, M. Boré had a host of imitators. He even attempted a great improvement—that of replacing the cane formerly cultivated in these regions with that from Tahiti. At the time he was expecting great advantages. Some were already apparent and unfailing. The cane from Tahiti ripens within eight to ten months, whereas the other requires twenty, twenty-four, thirty months; consequently, that from Tahiti does not have to risk the winters of lower Louisiana.[52]

Messrs. Fortier [Michel Fortier, aîné] and Godefroi [Godefroy Olivier de Vezin] have established a refinery. Sugar is more succulent here than in the Antilles. The cane is moister and contains less glucose. Refining costs 20 percent more than it costs in Saint-Domingue, but it yields an excellent grade of sugar. Since good farmland, properly mixed with clay, for sugar was deficient, they used to transport clay to the Cape [Cape Francais in Saint-Domingue] from the vicinity of Le Havre. Competition from Havana refiners is most detrimental to the refineries of New Orleans.

October 6—
The Hazeur
brothers

In October, I organized a trip on horseback along the Metairie road, toward the plantation of the three Hazeur brothers, real French knights from whom I had received many marks of kind attention. We made a journey of seven leagues and were back before noon. The day was delightful, the sky serene, and the breeze from the northeast cooled off the heat of the sun. Trees were still thick with foliage. Leaves fall so slowly in these countries. Evergreens, moreover, are abundant. Magnolias, vines, oaks, wild grapes, a great number of shrubs heavily laden with fruit—some pinkish, others violet, yellow, or black—all form a lovely sight deep in the heart of these uninhabited wastelands and forests. Sprinkled here and there are log cabins and some cultivation. And most everywhere it is alive with herds and multitudes of curious birds.

The sight of a well-kept plantation makes one envy its owner. Messrs. Hauser [Hazeur] possessed two such plantations, about three leagues from town. The oldest brother and the one they called "l'Habitant" lived together on one. The chevalier had his separate lodging on the other. They had only one shed, only one management, and only one income—they were models of brotherly closeness. They spent their days together. They had the same manners and the same tastes; even the tone of their voices was alike. They were not married. That was their shameful side, their colonial weakness; they were surrounded by offspring whose color betrayed their origin. Except for that, no others were better company, had a greater sense of honor or more loyalty, nor were more faithful Frenchmen. Born of a military family, they had themselves served in the regiments of our country. They *October* retired from it with the Cross of Saint Louis. They flared up in *31* anger at the very name of Spanish justice and American domination. French descendants were all more or less of that mettle.

A few days later, I invited them to my house for dinner, *Sunday,* bringing together with them a dozen or so of the most loyal, *November 6* the most distinguished Frenchmen whose hearts continued to cherish a tender affection for their mother country—the elite, in a word, of descendants of the first colonists. What a charming evening we spent! I chose a Sunday on purpose, to make sure to bring them together without inconveniencing any of them too much.

Sundays were generally observed as holidays. Everywhere there were many people and much coming and going. Some had dinner with relatives in the country; others arranged pleasure parties in the dance halls of the bayou. Whoever had a horse or a carriage was on the road. Strollers dressed in their Sunday finery were many. Young folks everywhere tried their skills— in one corner, they fired blank cartridges; elsewhere, they shot at birds. The Negroes and mulattoes, in groups of four, six, eight—some from the city, others from the country—challenged each other to *raquette des sauvages*.[53] I was invited to one of these contests, where bets rose from five to six hundred piastres fortes. Each team distinguished itself by ribbons of motley colors. The game was dangerous. Rarely did it happen that there were no accidents, no arms or legs broken. Metairie, more commonly called the Plaine Labarre, usually served as a tilting ground. The road was full with an unbroken line of traveling coaches, *cabriolets*, horses, carts, spectators, and players. The escorted winners retired triumphant. By a strange inconsistency, only too common, the spectators cheered and encouraged the skill and triumph of those very athletes whom they dreaded having to fight someday.

Hospitality The colonists are naturally confiding and hospitable! The hospitality of the Arabs is far less admirable. A ragged man, a sorry sight, appeared at nightfall at the Livaudais plantation where I was; they hurried to give him alms. When he asked for a place to sleep, "Ah! fine," said M. Livaudais, *père*, and he called out, "Take this man in." He was conducted to a little house destined for just such a purpose. M. Livaudais followed close behind and went to make sure that nothing was lacking. "Do you receive vagabonds so off-handedly?" I remarked to him. "That is our custom," he answered, "and until now, we have not had reason to regret it. What do you expect? These unfortunate people have to find a place to rest." The example that I witnessed is repeated every day on the plantations from one end of the colony to the other.

Slaves This feeling for humanity remains inert and dead when it comes to slaves. If exceptions exist, they are rare. The purpose of slavery is only to tie down the blacks so that they work the land like mules or oxen. To insure this result, there exists an organized hierarchy of drivers, chiefs, and overseers, always whip in hand. The work parties are called work gangs; they should be called teams [as teams of oxen rather than workmen in a shop]. Generally, one cannot expect fidelity, punctuality, or attachment. As a rule, a slave aims only to cheat his master, steal from him, and work as little as possible. They are sluggish, deceitful, and on the lookout for a chance to neglect their obligations with impunity. They know that for fear of losing them the master will not punish them, even for their most serious misdemeanors, except with a greater or lesser number of lashes or a couple of days in a lockup on bread and water.

These are the results of slavery—a detestable means that, no matter how you look at it, is not tantamount to sharecropping, renting, or other methods adopted by landowners to draw a profit from their properties. However, slavery does exist, and one can understand how it developed in the scorching climates of the tropics. Blind imitation of neighbors introduced it even into Louisiana. Since it does exist, it would be imprudent and unfair to wipe it out suddenly without long and judicious precautions. At least a vigilant and firm policing should ward off, or at least temper, its disadvantages, abuses, and dangers. Nothing of the sort existed at the time. A remnant of order was maintained in this respect by the force of habit and by the effect of local customs. Such are the reflections which this subject inspired in me concerning this country during my stay there.

I imagine that Saint-Domingue was, of all our colonies in the Antilles, the one whose mentality and customs influenced Louisiana the most. Frequent intercourse existed between the two. Even today when the Negroes, having become independent, have chased us from Haiti, exiles from the island prefer Louisiana as refuge. One meets many former settlers from there who had been given shelter in Louisiana by relatives and friends, and who, as a general rule, show neither affection nor kindness toward the blacks. A small number of Haitian slaves preferred to follow the fortunes of their impoverished masters rather than take a chance on the yield of their industry and labor or, in a word, rather than dire poverty. They populated Santiago de Cuba and numbered more

September 17

than six thousand. The governor, a Spanish officer of Irish birth, received them very well and offered them at low cost some small land grants on which they planted coffee. At the time of their flight from Saint-Domingue, they were tossed about from the Negroes to the English. These latter despoiled them of everything, even their clothes and their earrings. From Kingston, Jamaica, René Renaud, captain of the *Flore*, brought us seventy-two children, women, and aged men of distinguished families, once very rich.

And so I spent my days seeking to inform myself thoroughly about everything pertaining to a colony that France had founded a century ago and was about to launch into the ocean of American states. I waited impatiently to be sure about the news already too universally printed about and indicated by too many signs not to be true.[54]

August 18 – Official confirmation of cession of Louisiana to United States

At last, on the eighteenth of August, 1803, I received its confirmation from our *chargé d'affaires* in Washington, M. Pichon. This transfer was worth seventy-five million francs (fifteen million piastres fortes) to the First Consul. Spanish and French merchant ships would enjoy the advantages of the most favored nations; but France would lose a colony with a most beautiful future. While waiting for its emancipation, unavoidable in the course of time, we might have planted there an immense French population. That alone would have provided forever a wealthy resource and an outlet for the mother country. A new France might have been formed. Doubtless, powerful considerations and prudent diplomacy determined the cabinet at Saint-Cloud to make this sacrifice. It would have been difficult to guard Louisiana against attacks and intrigues from that England with whom we were beginning again an implacable war. On the contrary, with the cession of this colony, we fortified the United States, already a feared rival of the British Empire and added the most beautiful of its gems to the crown of the American Confederation.

Personally, I had hoped to spend six or eight years in an administration that would have at least doubled the population and agriculture of the country and tripled or quadrupled its trade, thus leaving behind a lasting and honorable memorial. Every day, I congratulated myself for having had this excellent idea and for having so well estimated the resources of this colony. I anticipated a time in the near future when every step I took would produce some good. I dreamed constantly of reform, improvement, and new establishment. The place, the inhabitants, the air—everything pleased me and offered facilities for my benevolent plans. All that vanished, leaving me only the regret of a year of idleness, of a useless migration by my family to the New World, and of many expenses, troubles, and fruitless inconveniences.

I expected final instructions from my government at any time. Another letter from M. Pichon reached me on the seventh of November notifying me that he would send me, by express, within eight or ten days, the official dispatches from Paris. I profited by the delay to visit the river banks some thirty or forty leagues upriver.

End of Book One

BOOK TWO

December, 1803 to July, 1804

I BEGAN MY ROUND of visits on horseback at the end of
November, 1803, accompanied by M. Charpin. We took the
road along the left bank of the Mississippi. M. Boré joined us
in front of his plantation. We lunched about four leagues
from town at the home of Madame Fortier, who was over
sixty years old, and we slept eight leagues farther up at the
home of M. d'Estrehan.

*Fortier,
la mère*

That day we skirted one cotton plantation, five general agriculture plantations, and twenty-seven sugar plantations,
nearly all belonging to respectable old Creole families. This
was the richest section of the colony. They were "grinding,"
as they say to describe the manufacturing of sugar at the
beginning of winter. The plantation where we lunched was
making its first attempt with Tahiti sugarcane imported into
Louisiana. They were delighted with it. The hydrometer [of
Baumé] was at 8½ degrees, which was considered quite favorable. The resulting sugar was very good.[1]

*Sugar
manufac-
turing*

About two or three leagues from the city, two Irish school
teachers known as the Meguy brothers conducted a boarding
school for eight pupils in a building intended for about
twenty-five. Also on this road lived M. Caberet [Pierre Marie
Cabaret d'Estrépy], one of the most respected of the old
settlers. He had just married a daughter to M. Robin de
Logny. "Let us celebrate the wedding night also," M. de
Logny said to his wife, and nine months later a charming
daughter was born, who is today thirteen or fourteen years
old.

*October–
November,
1803—
The Meguy
school
teachers*

Not far from M. Caberet lived the widow Eme [Marie Féli-
cité Julie Fortier Aime], a daughter of Fortier. She was very
beautiful. After childbirth, she took a chill which made her

blind. She went to Europe in order to consult doctors in London, Paris, and Montpellier. Dr. Portal told us that they tormented her with all sorts of cures and she came back still blind. They claimed a pregnancy would cure her, so she was going to give it a try with her uncle Fortier, and they were waiting for a dispensation from Rome.

M. d'Estrehan   We spent the night at the home [Ormond Plantation] of the most active and intelligent sugar planter of the colony. M. d'Estrehan has eight children, as many boys as girls, by his wife, who is a sister to Robin de Logny. In order to give an idea of the customs here, I will say that although she came from one of the first and wealthiest families in this colony, Madame d'Estrehan, together with her daughters, was looking after the salting and preserving of beef on this day. This was harvest season.

On this plantation, the Negroes were perfectly well kept. Each one cultivated his own little plot (his garden) with the master's encouragement. He bought clothes and such other articles as the slaves needed wholesale and resold them to the slaves without making a profit. It was to his advantage—his slaves were better clothed and did not run away. By a wise distribution of hours, M. d'Estrehan doubled the work of forty to fifty workers without overworking any of them.

He figured that his "grinding" would last two months this year, and would produce 250,000 pounds of sugar. He had been the first to fire up his furnace. His system was, first, to grind the frailer cane that was less resistant to frost, and then the sturdier. He helped with the cutting of the cane, an operation which he judged to be more important than was generally recognized. He divided his team of workers into "three-quarter watches" (an expression taken from the navy). The watches relieved each other every six hours. Most other sugar mills worked their slaves without stop for twelve to twenty-four hours. During grinding, the Negroes grew fat because the masters paid the food bill as long as they worked in the refinery.

In this country, only four kettles are generally used in refining. They do not use the so-called *propre* kettle, which brings

the cane juice to its highest degree of purity and crystalliza-
tion.[2] They use (1) the *grande,* into which the juice coming
from the mill that grinds the cane is conducted and under-
goes its first boiling; (2) the *flambeau,* which the refiner
watches for the sugarcane juice to give signs of boiling or of
sufficient lime content; (3) the *syrop,* in which the juice was
supposed to reach the consistency of syrup, but never did;
and finally (4) the *batterie,* in which the final cooking, called
cuite, causes a considerable bubbling, which is checked by
stirring the syrup vigorously with a skimming ladle.

In the Antilles, the fire in the sugar furnace is fed *bagasse,*
the stalk from the preceding year's cane as it comes from the
mill—crushed, drained of its juice, and dried. Having saved
some from last year for the first time, M. d'Estrehan assumed
he would use it up in two weeks. Up until now, this colony
had used wood for its sugar firing. Since wood will become
scarce in time, M. d'Estrehan has set an example that others
will follow. There is no denying, however, that *bagasse* will
never have the bulk in this climate that it has in the tropical
regions.[3]

For the sugar refiners, grinding is the most important operation. It causes them extreme worry, especially in Louisiana,
where they supervise the work themselves instead of trusting
an overseer. M. d'Estrehan was there all the time, following
all of the operations. Woe to anyone who would disturb one
of his Negroes at this time, or his horses, or oxen! Obliging
though he usually was, this would have been like stabbing
him in the back. One sugar mill was estimated to cost anywhere between ten and fifteen thousand piastres fortes, not
including the wood or the bricks which were cut or fabricated
on the plantation.

We received the most cordial hospitality. This parish (that
is what they call a commune) is that of the Germans, or of
Saint-Charles. The social status of the parish priests at the
time was not very respectable. Adventurers, gluttons, drunk-
ards, often unfrocked monks, they were asked but one thing
by their parisioners—that they be, as was said, "good na-
tured." Churches are built on one or the other bank of the

river, about ten leagues apart, so that a parish extends five leagues around in all directions on both sides from the waterfront. Each curé enjoyed a nice presbytery, a fenced-in plot of ground, and an annual salary of thirty or forty piastres fortes. Moreover, parishioners showed a great kindness for the curé.

November 11

On Thursday, the eleventh of November, M. Charpin and I breakfasted with the d'Estrehan family and left about eight o'clock. The second plantation we passed was that of the widow Trépanier [Pierre Trépagnier]. Three years earlier, she had been witness to a horrible tragedy. The following account gives a fair notion of Spanish justice in the colonies. A colonist, whose name I refrain from mentioning, set his mind on marrying Mlle Trépanier.[4] Her father preferred M. Villeboeuf [Jean de la Villebeuvre], whom she later married. The colonist regarded the father as the principal obstacle to his plans. One night, someone asked for Trépanier at his door, and he was never seen alive again.[5] A few days later, his body was exhumed, and it was verified that he had been murdered. Rumor put a name on the murderer, who had been seen at two or three o'clock the day after the fatal night. Coming back into town with a comrade, he was disheveled and covered with mud, and his clothes were rumpled. Well-known witnesses were not questioned, but witnesses who would provide an alibi were produced, and the case was soon hushed up. Nevertheless, the indignation of neighbors and the general public was aroused. The Spanish commanders, who, while maintaining a passive role, hardly concealed their own anger, nonetheless admitted the accused to their holiday celebrations.

An example of Spanish justice

We pushed ahead along seventeen cotton plantations and five sugar plantations. Only two of these sugar mills are important enough to produce sugar; the others make *guildive* [*tafia*]. On some of the plantations that grow cotton, both rice and indigo are also cultivated. We stopped at the last of the sugar mills, that of M. Andri [Manuel Andry], and had dinner with Madame Andri, he being absent. M. Andri was the commanding officer of his parish, called the Second German Coast or Saint-Jean-Baptiste, whose church is situated on the right bank of the river. Our noonday meal was delayed a little for a good enough reason—they served us a banquet!

The eldest son in the household, who was seventeen or eighteen years old, had married the evening before Mademoiselle Glapiant [Catherine Sophie de Glopion], thirteen or fourteen years old. Early marriages are frequent in these parts. The children here, in this particular case, had been asking to be married for the past two years, and the parents gave in. Madame Andri was none too pleased, fearing that such a youthful daughter-in-law would make her look older.

After a jovial dinner, we set out again at one-thirty in the afternoon. We passed seven or eight rice, indigo, and corn plantations and lodged for the night at the home of M. Lebourgeois [Louis Le Bourgeois], a cotton planter. From M. Andri's house to there was almost nothing but Germans or Alsatians, who were well off.

M. Lebourgeois, born near Caen, had joined one of his uncles at Laréole; from there, he often hawked his wares in Pau, Nay, and Béarn. Then he moved to Louisiana, where he married the younger Sardey's widow. They have settled on this farm and prosper fairly well. There are nine children in the Lebourgeois family; eight in that of M. d'Estrehan. Ten or twelve is not uncommon, and eighteen to twenty astonishes no one. Second and third marriages are also very common. Yet, what vast wilderness still remains to be populated!

It was a curious sight to see fifty or sixty turkeys at sundown perched pyramid-like one above the other to the very top of a pecan tree; I was inclined to take it for a tree loaded with large fruit, a sort of turkey tree. That Friday, November 11, we had breakfast before leaving and were back in the saddle at seven-thirty, in the company of M. Lebourgeois.

The eighteen to twenty plantations and farms that we found as far as the *éboulis* [landslides of the river banks] were small cotton and rice plantations and truck farms run by Germans and Acadians. The *éboulis* are so called because of the frequent *éboulemens* [land cave-ins] to which the river banks are subject, causing the river road to be cut a little farther inland through the woods.

At this point, that is, a short half league from the Lebourgeois plantation, begins the Longue Vue de la Ramée. The Mississippi is the most winding of rivers, but here it flows extraordinarily straight for a stretch of two leagues. For a long time the Duparcs [Dupards] have owned a vast land grant in this spot, which was looked after by a Negro known as La Ramée. That was the origin of the name Longue Vue de la Ramée. The dense woods contained copaiba, live oak, pecan and the like, and thick vines. Sixty head of cattle coming from the Atakapas passed right in front of us, heading for the meat markets in town.

I wanted to see one of those Acadian families which populated this coast. So I went to the house of Pierre Michel, a cotton and corn planter. He and his wife are sexagenarians. Both born in Acadia, they were married in Louisiana and had seven or eight children. Everybody in the house was at work—one daughter was ironing; another was spinning; and the mother was distributing the cotton, while a number of little Negroes, all under twelve, were carding it, picking out the seeds, and drying it. No one, more than these people, regretted not being able to remain French.

When, in 1755, Acadia was conquered by the English, the French colonists there refused to swear allegiance to the conquerors and, consequently, were forced to leave their native country. Louisiana, doomed in a few years to pass under Spanish domination, received them. Some of the Acadians came directly, and some came by way of France; some came at their own expense, and others at the expense of the government. Most of them settled on this coast, to which they gave their name Côte-des-Acadiens, and the rest settled at La Fourche.[6] The last arrivals in Louisiana were brought here from France by Spain about twenty years ago. Like the Germans or the Alsatians, their neighbors on these shores, they are a hardworking and industrious people. Their morals are loose, and they are a very handsome species of men. They cultivate cotton, corn, and rice on seventeen or eighteen small farms, which follow one after the other. These farms lead to the large cotton plantation of M. [Marius Pons] Bringier, where we were expected for the night.

We were nearly there when, at the height of the day's heat, we came upon a pretty, slender young lady riding a horse and dressed with elegant simplicity, a straw hat on her head. "Isn't that," we said to her by way of opening a conversation, "the house of M. Bonaventure Gaudin?" She answered, "No, sir. You have just passed it." We then asked, "Are we far from the house of M. Bringier?" She said, "I don't know," and proceeded on her way. "Surely you are from M. Bonaventure Gaudin's household," we said. "No." And she galloped away resolutely. This wood nymph in the heart of these solitary forests—her youth, her elegance, her beauty, the way she rode—provided momentary and pleasant amusement on our trip. Upon dismounting, we learned that she was a Creole, thirteen or fourteen years old, who was married six months ago.

The house where we stayed offered another more striking example of the marriage customs in these lonely regions. A second-rate dauber in paints by the name of Colomb, who fancied himself a descendant of that illustrious navigator, went in 1788 from Paris, where he was born, to the United States. Coming down to New Orleans, he stopped at the home of M. Bringier in order to paint his apartments. Here he married the daughter of his host.[7] Marriages in the smartest families are not arranged otherwise, and Colomb was installed in the home as a son. M. Tureau [Augustin-Dominique Tureaud], husband of a sister of Madame Colomb, was associated with M. Bringier and managed his stores in the city.[8]

M. Bringier, a native of Provence [and a merchant], set out in search of adventure in Martinique; he lived there for four years, entrusting to one of his brothers a trading ship he was having sent to Louisiana. Not hearing any word of it, he came to Louisiana, did not find it (it was most probably lost at sea), and settled here.

So long as the English possessed the Floridas and Manchac, or the left bank of the Mississippi, they furnished these people, notably the Acadians and Germans, with merchandise and even slaves. M. Bringier arrived about the time when the English were expelled from here, during the war in the American colonies. He took over their trade and made money. A considerable stretch of fallow land was granted to him. On it he built up this superb plantation and operated simultaneously his cultivations and his business. His store here is still worth 20,000 to 25,000 piastres fortes; but today he has to contend with three or four competitors.

The house that he built for himself is the most substantial, the best constructed, best appointed, and most distinguished of the country houses in the colony [White Hall Mansion]. The roof forms an Italian terrace with a balustrade all around it. The interior arrangement lacks taste and comfort. The exterior buildings speak of work, industry, and affluence; here are seen corn and cotton mills, presses, etc. These mills are run by horses. Lower Louisiana does not have a single water mill. We enjoyed a good fare, as was usual with the colonists who produce on their lands everything they serve.

I went to bed intending to push some twenty leagues farther the next day, even as far as M. [Allard] Duplantier's home in Baton Rouge. I was therefore most disturbed by the noisy and stormy downpour that I heard during the night. When I awoke, the horizon was unusually overcast, and I postponed my departure until the next day. A continuous rain gutted the roads. Against my will I had to consent to go back on the second day by way of the river in a boat which M. Bringier offered me.

November 13

Courier service established between New Orleans and

While I was on Bringier's plantation, an Anglo-American from Nantuky [Natchez] arrived with four horses. He was a
. contractor who, by orders from the president of the United States, came to establish the relays for a new courier service between Natchez and New Orleans. A voluntary subscription from private individuals had established an earlier one, even though the Spanish government had not wished to cooperate; but that courier service took forty days from here to Washington City. Now, the trip between Natchez and New Orleans will be made in less than four days, and from

Natchez to Washington City will take two weeks. Thus letters from the capital of the United States will get to New Orleans in less than twenty days. There is the first benefit of the union. Established at this location, the relay station will cost only fifteen piastres fortes per month for food and maintenance.[9]

Natchez for correspondence with Washington City in nineteen days

Fortified with a wholesome breakfast, Messrs. Bringier, Charpin, and I set out in a boat maneuvered by four Negro oarsmen. The river was at its lowest; consequently, the very high banks prevented us from seeing the plantations at close range. We passed seven cotton plantations on our right. Among them was the plantation of M. [Jean-Baptiste Poeyfarré] Poeyferré, a Béarnais from Castetner near Maslacq who, by his excellent reputation in this remote country, brings honor to our common fatherland.

Departure for New Orleans by river

In three hours we landed at the plantation of M. [Michel Bernard de Cantrille] Canterelle, in the parish of Saint James [in the region of the] Cabahonacés (in the language of the Indians, duck country), where he was commanding officer.

Cabahonacés

I have said that a parish includes both river banks for five leagues around. Since today was Sunday, the parishioners were just returning home from mass, some in boats which ferried them across the river, others in groups of men and women on horseback, galloping away together.

I already knew this worthy and distinguished gentleman, M. de Canterelle; I had received four *canards branchus* [wood ducks] from him. His wife was the sister of Andri and Sosten [Gilbert Sosthène Andry, brother of Bernard-Noël Andry and of Celeste Andry].

At once a picture of a typical Louisiana plantation struck me. Five or six strangers enjoying the hospitality strolled along the gallery. I will point out M. Montanvert as a perfect example of the type of adventurer who abounds in this colony. A Savoyard from a good family, he was destined at first for the priesthood; but political events cast him upon these shores instead, where he made, lost, and recovered a fortune. He started out as a peddler and made the rounds of the posts. He bought a pack mule and continued his hawking. Then he

M. Montanvert

bartered the mule for a scow and navigated back and forth across the lakes, bayous, and river. Soon he was master of a schooner and went to Campêche, where his goods were confiscated as being smuggled, leaving him penniless. He did not become discouraged, but came back and started all over again as he had done the first time. He was chatty, honest, friendly, and welcomed by everybody.

Canterelle sugar mill

The sugar mill of M. de Canterelle and the rest of his buildings were, I believe, the finest and best arranged in Louisiana. There was a lumber mill besides. The land was among the most extensive of plantation lands. A bayou irrigated it.

The Cabahonacés, or rather the Oumes [Houmas], an Indian tribe, formerly lived there. Ten or twelve families survived until a few years ago. At the time four families remained, two of which I saw. They were just like a part of the Canterelle household.[10] They spoke Choctaw and French. All of these Indians are disappearing—rum and the Americans exterminate them.

We had our midday meal at two o'clock and sat at the table for some time. How much pepper! What highly seasoned food! But especially how much pepper! Real fire, this food of Louisiana!

Oranges

On the left bank of the river, the sweet orange does not do very well beyond the Andri plantation. The bitter or sour orange is found even below Pointe-Coupée, on the right bank of the river. The sweet orange grows very near the Canterelle plantation, but it can hardly withstand the freezes. Rice growing hardly extends above the river bank cave-in areas; corn and cotton follow thereafter. It is generally admitted that in lower Louisiana the right bank of the river is warmer than the left, and that the winds coming from the northwest become balmier as they pass over the Mississippi.

Illiterate inhabitants

On all of these shores very few inhabitants are able to write or even read. There was a Swiss, a schoolteacher in the first German parish, called Saqué. He was 103 years old and had gotten drunk regularly every day for the past forty years.

I got back into the boat a little late. We saw clouds of duck

and teal flying overhead in all directions and on either side of *Flights*
us, some of them continuing on their course straight ahead, *of lake*
others pausing on the surface of the water. We noticed that *birds*
some plunged directly into the water and never came up to
the surface again. At every quarter-league, hunters, either in
pirogues or on the shore, were on the lookout, and echoes
were heard far off, repeating the gunshots.

It was six-thirty when we entered the house of M. Armand
[Jean Marie Armant]. The river banks were not easily accessi-
ble. One of our Negroes got out of the boat and, shortly after,
announced the end of our search, pointing out a place where
we climbed quite easily up the shore, with the help of a large
amount of cotton seeds that had been spread on the bank.
The table was set. A neighbor, the father, the son-in-law, and
daughter-in-law stood around the candlelight, and the
mother soon came in. We felt entirely a part of the family
here. Nothing was changed at the table; they simply added
two more places. Three-quarters of an hour later dinner was
served. These are inhabitants of Nakitoches transplanted
here; they spoke of Nakitoches as the haven of a golden age.
We were placed comfortably in a room with two very clean
beds and a beautiful porcelain bowl on our table. We had
breakfast with the family and we reembarked.

After having edged past three sugar mills and five cotton
plantations, we had dinner at the home of M. [Daniel] Pain, *November 14—*
some 6½ leagues from our starting point. He came to this *M. Pain;*
country as a surgeon of a Swiss regiment in the service of *hunting in*
France. A vigorous sexagenarian, he was the most intrepid *Louisiana*
hunter in all of Louisiana. His great hunting party began early
in December and lasted three weeks. The expedition took in
all of the area around Lake Malin and La Grand Prairie. His
camp is on the little hill of Denné, about six leagues from his
house, to the rear and up as far as the Massico (Geneviève
Grevenberg) [Mme Jacques B. Massicot] plantation. His wife
went along and salted, or, according to the expression in the
country, marinated, innumerable quantities of ducks. Those
are days of reunion and great fun. Friends come from fifteen
or twenty leagues around to visit and hunt. They eat plenty of

game, oysters, and fish. They push out into the whole maze of bayous and lakes, which have yet to be charted and in which only those familiar with the area know how to find their way.

These hunting parties are a rage. The Louisianian has acquired and maintained this penchant for hunting from the Indians, and he rarely misses his target. Folks from town go to Lake Barataria for these hunting parties, which usually last a week or two.

People were already beginning to eat nothing else but snipe, teal, and all kinds of duck, etc. Even that morning as we were coming down the river, in cloudy and foggy weather, we met continual flocks of birds in flight or playing on the river. M. Pain urged me to come along and enjoy his great hunt; he promised that I would have a good time. Having been seated at his table and having shared his noon meal, we cut our visit short and left after dinner, at one-thirty, for we were anxious not to have to look around for night lodging along the way.

Thus far along the river the staple crop had been rice. From here on, we proceeded downstream from sugar mill to sugar mill. It was really interesting and picturesque to see so many furnaces, one after the other, belching clouds of curling black smoke that were ablaze at times. This spectacle entertained us as we came down the river and provided the milestones by which we gauged our progress. Thus, we were led to the home of M. Abine [Louis Habiné], the second husband of Madame Fortier. He was home alone. We spent the evening like bachelors, talking about sugar and Béarn. He was born in Barlest, near Pontacq. From his gallery, which extends all around the house, one could see at night on the river bank the smoking furnaces of the d'Estrehans, Esnes, Labranches, and seven or eight others in all directions.

Descending the river lighted by the fires of sugar mills

Bad weather caught up with us the next day, with a north wind, rain, and a surging river. The sail propelled us forward and soon drove us back. We tacked from point to point and, in this way, frequently crossed over from one side to the other. We traversed these joltings. In this season, the river-

November 15— Accidents on the river

banks were remarkable for their height and for the numerous land cave-ins which inconvenience and sometimes ruin and discourage those who live along the river. Prior to these accidents, the levee gave way several fathoms, always causing heavy expenses. The inhabitants consider themselves fortunate when a batture begins to form or continues to build up in front of their land. But one bank builds up firmly only at the expense of the opposite bank, and a batture always means a bank cave-in; one is always in proportion to the other. [11] At a glance, on a cross section of ten, twelve, fifteen, twenty feet or more, these cave-ins seem to be layers of heavy compost, apparently coming from the surrounding deposits; but at eight or ten feet, this layer loses its blackish color and takes on a yellowish gray color.

At the time, the Mississippi was like a magnificent, long, stretched-out lake. One sailed up the river with just about the same ease with which one descended it. It was little traveled because its bayous and its other connecting channels either were dry or had very little water. We did not meet four boats. On the other hand, we passed pirogues of every size. The smallest ones held only one person. From their youth, the inhabitants paddled out in them, running through the waves or passing over them.

Continuing our navigation along the river during this day, we were somewhat slowed down by the swelling waters and the winds; but we arrived at M. Duparc's [François Dupard's] plantation, across from a few truck farms and three sugar mills. He had given me too many marks of personal esteem and signs of attachment to France for me to pass him by. Every day, for the past forty years, he had written down the events that attracted his attention, differing in this respect from other colonials, who remained indifferent to passing events.

M. Duparc

Colas, who had waited on me three months ago at the time of my arrival, immediately bustled about to prepare lunch. Anyone wishing to get an idea of a Louisiana bachelor should come to this place. M. Duparc was born into a considerable fortune. His father was an example of the colonial prospects for the hard-working emigrant. He came to Mobile as a shoemaker and, as a shoemaker, moved to New Orleans. There he set up a business, increased his fortune, and bought a fine piece of land, part of which belongs to his son. There he placed some Negroes for whom he paid six hundred francs a head to the Company of the Indies, and he raised their number to more than one hundred. He had four daughters whom he endowed handsomely and married into the best families.[12] The son was neither a hunter, a soldier, nor a man-about-town. He read and scribbled down notes; his room—his study—contained only scattered papers and books.

Duparc had a great number of excellent slaves, but he neither sowed nor harvested with them. He borrowed to live and to keep them alive, and he bought their garments but did not receive pay for them. M. Duparc was reduced to emergency measures. Although recently obliged to give up several Negroes to meet the demands of his creditors, he still had a good number. His head slaves were more masters of the house than he himself. As soon as we appeared, two little mulatto girls and one little mulatto boy, very nice and between the ages of nine and sixteen, changed the linen, set the table, and prepared the service. They lavished attentions on us, waited upon us, and courteously foresaw all of our needs. They were, one guessed, the children of the master of the house. Toward noon, we returned to our boat, and that day was already noted down in M. Duparc's album.

Sawmills We passed a score of plantations, among which five were sugar, one was cotton, a dozen or thirteen others were truck farms and corn fields, and four were sawmills. These mills are called "sawmills" in this country because they are used for little other than making planks, with which Louisiana supplies Havana. This trade alone was worth 200,000 piastres fortes. A good "miller," as they say, received eight to ten thousand piastres fortes from his mill during its operation— from the fifteenth of December, during the season of high water, to May or June, when the water is so low that the mills can no longer saw.

The bank on the approaches to the city was populated with people whom I have seen in New Orleans or elsewhere—the Lebretons from Organnois [d'Orgenois], whose brother is a brigadier general that I met at the home of M. de Pontalba; [Jean-Baptiste de] Fleuriaus, one of whose daughters is married to Dugué-Livaudais and who gave shelter to the refugee Marmé from Saint-Domingue; Dominique Bouligni [Bouligny], who is from a fine family and is industrious in more than one line; St. Dée [Pierre St. Pé], who is a nephew of M. Livaudais, père, and a son-in-law of M. de Villars, another refugee from Saint-Domingue, who possessed wit, culture, and sophistication; Robin Delogny, who is one of the most active residents and who supplied New Orleans with vegetables that earned him 2,500 piastres fortes that year. At the time, he was in Pointe-Coupée, seeing to some cypress trees for his mill and intending to bring back a hundred good milk cows.

We were across from the elder Marigny plantation. High as the batture was, so correspondingly deep and eroding was the Bernoudy *écore* on the opposite bank. We had only to allow ourselves to drift along and cross over in front of the *November* city to land at the point where we began our trip. I got out *24* there and was happy to be back again with my family and in the midst of my pressing affairs.

In fact, almost immediately, I received from M. Trask, an American, a dispatch, which he handed to me on behalf of M. [William C. C.] Claiborne from Natchez. It was from M. Pichon, our minister plenipotentiary to the United States. He notified me of the imminent arrival of M. [Pierre] Landais, whom he was sending to bring me, from Washington City, the dispatches addressed to me by my government for the cession of Louisiana.

On the evening of the same day, November 24, 1803, I began to play my part. General [James] Wilkinson, commissioner appointed to join M. Claiborne and to receive Louisiana from my hands, came from Mobile and stopped on his way to Fort Adams. He wished to meet me and become acquainted.[13] Heavy, squat, good-natured, talkative, and open-faced, he hardly understood the French language. We went into my office where I informed him of the news which had just reached me and of my situation as a result. We agreed that he would apply himself to the matter as diligently as possible.

December
4

Just as he was leaving, M. Landais entered the room and handed me the letters from France. M. Landais was the son of a Frenchman who, having to flee from Fort Dauphin in Saint-Domingue because of the Marquis de Casacalvo's strictness, sought refuge in Louisiana at the home of his friend Faurie. From there, he went to fill a post given to him by Admiral Villaret as notary public in Martinique. He left his two sons in the United States. One of them is the very man whom M. Pichon sent to me.

After M. Landais came M. Lyons [James Lyon], director of

Lyons

the *Gazette gouvernementale de la Nouvelle-Orléans* [*Orleans Gazette*]. He was a zealous federalist, who came here to establish a newspaper under the auspices of the government.

I am assigned
to the prefecture
of Martinique

The dispatches from France notified me, under the seal of secrecy, that after I had fulfilled the mission with which I was charged in Louisiana, I was assigned the colonial prefecture of Martinique. They had certainly not consulted me.[14]

Meetings with
the Spanish
commissioners

I received my packet of letters on December 4 [November 24] and on the fifth [November 25] I had a meeting with the Spanish commissioners. I gave them a letter from my government. We agreed on the retrocession. I was offered the service of the troops of His Catholic Majesty. I refused it. The Marquis de Casacalvo concluded from this that I would therefore name a commander of militia, and I did not deny it.

Dispositions
for the
retrocession

I had already started a movement among my friends to attract into my circle some Louisianians whom I wanted to use. More than anything else, I needed as commander a soldier who was knowledgable and firm, and I needed a respected mayor. For the first, I decided upon M. Deville-Depontin-

Commander
of militia

Bellechasse [Joseph de Ville de Goutin Bellechasse], a former officer of the Mexican Regiment. He had obtained his retirement under hardly favorable conditions because of the intrigues of the Marquis de Casacalvo, whom he had defied. For

the second, I had my eye on M. Boré, a wealthy, indus- *Mayor and*
trious settler, who never flinched before the Spanish officials *municipal*
and who had a well-earned reputation for patriotism and *council*
integrity.

I assured myself of the capabilities of these men. Once I
had won them over by my entreaties and my insistence, sup-
ported principally by their own interests and those of their
country, I proceeded to set up a good municipal council. I
wanted some merchants, some Americans, and some experienced businessmen. I intended to bear in mind and to honor
the memory of the Frenchmen who had been sacrificed under
O'Reilly. I looked about for a secretary registrar who might
make this political machine function—one who might be its
soul and who might have honesty, talent, diplomacy, and
popularity. In other words, I wanted a municipality so constructed that it would do me honor and hold its own with
dignity before the Americans upon their arrival and after they
had taken possession. This being the dominant act of my
short-lived reign and the one to which I attached the greatest
importance because of its possible long-term consequences
for the future of Louisiana, I set down my choices at this
point:

MAYOR:
Boré
SECRETARY REGISTRAR:
Derbigny
FIRST DEPUTY (who will be provisionally the first assistant to
the mayor):
Destrehan
SECOND DEPUTY:
Sauvé
MUNICIPAL COUNCIL:
Livaudais, père
Petit-Cavelier
Villeray (Jacques Philippe Vileré), worthy son of him
(Joseph) who was judicially assassinated by O'Reilly
Johns, Sr. [Evan Jones], a wealthy American and a
naturalized Spaniard of long standing

Fortier, père
Donaldson (a much-respected and much-loved American)
Faurie (a merchant with a great fortune)
Allard, fils (member of a very esteemed family; he was only twenty-three years old, but intelligent, self-confident, and ambitious)
Tureaud (merchant, son-in-law to Bringier, and one of the best businessmen in New Orleans)
John Watkins (an American physician, capable and honest)
TREASURER:
Labatut (a respectable and respected gentleman from Bayonne).[15]

On the evening of that same day, the Marquis de Casacalvo and the secretary of the Spanish government, Don Andrés Lopez de Armesto, returned the draft of the proceedings I had submitted to them. It remained as set down, except for a few insignificant corrections they made. The marquis spoke to me about boundary lines [of the province]. I replied that I would transfer the country according to the terms of the treaty [of San Ildefonso, signed between France and Spain on October 1, 1800], and not concern myself at all with the application of these terms, a matter that Spain would straighten out with the United States.[16] I let him know the points which my instructions designated as frontiers on the east, south, west, and north.

Boundary lines

He spoke to me again about the troops with which I intended to take possession in the name of the Republic, and he proposed once again that I combine with these the troops and officers of His Catholic Majesty. I refused categorically.[17] Next he asked me what I was planning to do about the *cabildo*; I answered that I was going to establish a new municipal body. Although naturally secretive as Spaniards generally are when they think they have experience in, or some idea of, government, he let his pent-up anger flash through his smile. We parted at nine o'clock in the evening, entirely in agreement.

Refusal of aid of the Spanish troops and of their militia in taking possession of the colony

On the following evening, I called together at my house the members of the new municipal council, and I made known my views with regard to them. I explained the designs of France in the treaty [of cession signed on April 30, 1803, with the United States] and the advantages of the treaty to them. I made it plain that I could easily have dispensed with the trouble I was giving myself and that it might have been more convenient for me personally to make use of the existing political body in order to receive and transfer the colony, but that I had intended to render a great service to the Louisianians and to give them a signal proof of the attachment and the interest they had inspired in me. I wanted them to profit from my flash of power and influence in handing over to them the fortress, as it were, and admitting into it a select few from among their number. I told them where I stood on all points and read my various decrees to them. I called upon them to accept or reject the offices with which I was investing them, and I arranged a meeting with them for the following day at the prefecture.[18] I promised to install them in turn after the colony had been handed over to me. In all of this, there were some buts, ifs, and fors, which I had either to get around or to defeat.

The thorniest article concerned the militia, the only real military force at my disposal. I requested the Spanish commissioners to assemble it for the ceremony. I warned them that, since their general staff was in the pay of the king of Spain, I would replace it immediately, as the first of my actions. This decision did not please either the Spaniards or the general staff. I was compelled, however, to call upon the Spanish administration to have the militia assembled. I knew that for the past forty-eight hours they secretly plotted to deter the militia from serving on this occasion and to cause trouble for France and myself. I opposed with some countermoves, but I did not have by far the advantage of position.

In the morning, I learned that M. Andri Sosten [Gilbert Sosthène Andry], the Spanish colonel of the militia and a brave and gallant gentleman who was indebted for his promotion to the Marquis de Casacalvo, had said to the assembled militia, "See if you want to serve the French Republic for two weeks." He came at ten-thirty to acquaint me with the difficulties he was having with the militia in spite of his efforts. I answered him flatly: "Sir, I know what it means to act one way openly to meet one's responsibility and another way secretly for one's satisfaction. I am not a child; I am not to be deceived by mere words. I do not accuse you. Assure M. le marquis however, that I know this country and its people too well now not to understand perfectly who is to blame if the militia fails me. The French government will know it also, just as I do."

After that, he renewed officially, in the name of the marquis, the proposition that I use the militia and, as auxiliaries, even the Spanish troops. And so endlessly they turned round and round the same trap in order to ensnare me. This time, I pushed it aside firmly and indignantly.

M. Sosten bustled about excitedly. There were 250 men under arms, among whom was the entire company of grenadiers [the Spanish Regiment of Louisiana] in uniform. On my part, I did not neglect things either. I had called forth an assembly from a multitude of French citizens, the greater number of whom had borne arms during the Revolution. They procured guns and sabers for themselves. Clark [Daniel Clark, Jr.] had likewise assembled Americans throughout the morning. They had organized themselves into companies and had appointed him their captain. He came to offer me their services. [19]

At 11:45, on the morning of November 30, 1803, I set out on foot for the city hall [The Cabildo], escorted by approximately sixty Frenchmen. [20] The brig *Argo* fired a salute as we passed. We arrived at the Place [d'Armes, now known as Jackson Square]. The crowd there was considerable. The Spanish troops were standing at attention on one side, the militia on the other. The drums rolled in front of the guardroom when I passed. The commissioners of H.C.M. came midway across the room to meet me. M. de Salcedo sat down in the armchair in the middle, I sat in another on his right, and the Marquis de Casacalvo sat in a third to his left. I presented my creden-

Taking
possession

tials and the order from the king of Spain. The secretary, Don Andrés Lopez de Armesto, was given the order to read the powers of his nation's commissioners, and upon my order [Joseph] Daugerot, clerk of the navy, read my appropriate powers. The Marquis de Casacalvo formally announced that subjects who did not choose to remain under the Spanish dominion were, from that moment on, rightfully released from their oath of allegiance. At the same time, the governor handed me, on a silver tray, the keys to Fort Saint Charles and Fort Saint Louis. Thereupon he relinquished his place to me, and I accepted it.

Don Andrés read in Spanish the official proceedings of the cession as agreed upon and transcribed in advance, and immediately thereafter Daugerot read the French version. We signed and affixed the seals. Then we rose and went out on the side of the balconies of the city hall. Upon our appearance, the Spanish flag, which had been flying atop the flagstaff, was lowered, and the French flag was raised. The company of grenadiers of the Spanish Regiment of Louisiana went forward to take the Spanish flag, and the Spanish troops filed off after it in double time.

The commissioners of H.C.M. moved toward the door to leave; I followed them as far as the top of the stairs. The secretaries of our commission and our staff officers accompanied them as far as the foot of the stairs where their secretaries had received us. Poor old Salcedo was collapsing from decrepitude. The Marquis de Casacalvo maintained all the while that calm and serene appearance which even the most second-rate politicians of his nation never lose.

As soon as they had marched off, I descended into the Place [d'Armes]. I took my place in the middle of the front line of the militia, which was standing in battle formation. M. Sosten was there. Addressing me, he said that he had reassembled them according to my wishes and that he was turning them over to me. I thanked him. I proclaimed M. Bellechasse as their commander and delivered a short speech praising him. I ordered the decree to be read, and I charged them to recognize him as their commander and to obey him in everything that he would order for the public service. Lastly, I added: "In the name of the French Republic, I entrust these flags to you. You shall defend them; you shall honor them. They are raised in your midst for the good of your country; they are here as they are in their native land. French blood is in the veins of most of you." During this ceremony, cannons thundered on all sides.

Having returned home, I occupied myself with receiving reports and giving orders to counteract the ill will and inactivity with which the Spanish leaders had sought to embarrass my assuming of authority. Above all, I rallied the militia to the colors by stirring up the leaders a little and by completing the general staff. The next day, I drew up plans to observe a French flag day with dinner, concert, ball, and supper. I issued my orders and sent out my invitations.

Urgent decrees and the prompt reorganization of the militia were my first acts of business for the next day. It had been impossible to change the entire guard on that day, but that never happened again.

I received visitors—the intendant, the governor, and the marquis, together with a brilliant retinue; the chief military staff; and the clergy—all of whom arrived on foot at my house. About a quarter of an hour later, I, in turn, went to the governor's house; the company that had followed him reassembled there; I was accompanied by a countless number of members of the new government. The remainder of the day was one continuous holiday. Seventy-five people came for dinner—as many Spaniards as Americans and Frenchmen—and began gambling before dinner. They did not stop gambling without incurring great losses, and without all sorts of tomfoolery; and they continued until eight o'clock the next morning. Two sumptuous servings were interrupted by three toasts—the first was made with a white champagne, to the French Republic and to Bonaparte; the second, with a pink champagne, to Charles IV and to Spain; the third, with a white champagne, to the United States and to Jefferson. Each of these toasts was accompanied by three salvos of twenty-one guns fired from the batteries of La Porte de la Prefecture,

St. Charles, and the French brig, the *Argo*. It was getting late as we drank a noisy toast to the ladies and we rose.

Coffee was hardly served when crowds of people began to come inside. The unsettled weather of the night before had cleared, and a gust of north wind, the most piercing of winter, had dried the earth and brought out the stars. The wind blew fiercely, upsetting some of the lighting, particularly around the city hall and the prefecture. Nevertheless, the huge fire pots lit up both the entrances and the front premises with a glowing light.

A hundred women attended, most of them beautiful or pretty and all of them well built, elegant, and gorgeously dressed. One hundred fifty to two hundred men moved in and out in three lively quadrilles, while card tables were set up everywhere. They danced in a flood of lights within the various rooms, whose doors I had ordered taken down. English quadrilles interrupted every third French one.[21] To open the ball, the Marquis de Casacalvo danced a minuet with Madame [Louise de la Ronde] Almonaster. Some spirited dances by M. Folck [Vincente Folch y Juan] and M. Dugay of Bordeaux followed. Finally, they mixed in some waltzes. Madame Livaudais and Madame Boré, who had given up balls years ago, revived their taste for them on this occasion.

We had supper at three o'clock in the morning. There were two tables; the large one seated fifty-five persons and the small one, twenty. The guests did justice to the meal. The dances began all over again. Little by little, the gentlemen and ladies took their leave. At five o'clock, however, two quadrilles were still in full swing. At seven o'clock, the *danse des bateaux* and *galopade* were still holding forth, and eight persons were still dancing when the last gamblers broke up their game.

On December 2, I appointed the captain of the frigate *Léonard* as commander of Plaquemines, and I placed under him at La Balise M. Olivier, a lieutenant commander on half-pay. M. Rives, a lieutenant commander on half-pay, was selected as commander of Fort Saint John. All of them left

Friday, December 2

Diverse government measures

their positions at the head of some troops to take possession of their posts. Then I devoted myself to an act of justice that the representative of the French government owed the colony, both as tribute and as an example.

M. Dublanc [Louis Charles de Blanc] was a good man, born

Saint-Julien affair at Atakapas

in Nakitoches and descended on his maternal side from M. de Saint-Denis. He left Nakitoches twenty-five years ago and moved to Atakapas, where M. de Galvés named him commandant. He went to New Orleans last April, as he generally did, and he learned from the commandant of Côte-des-Allemands that, by an agreement between the government and myself, we were working on a census. He wrote to his post to have them proceed with it, and he entrusted [Pierre-Louis de] Saint-Julien with his letter. Saint-Julien was a Frenchman whom I knew in New Orleans and who gave me some personal observations. This Saint-Julien returned home. Because he was an intelligent man, he took it upon himself to do the job in his district. He had a keen imagination and a carefree character. Perhaps, when speaking with him, I had put some wrong notions into his head about French domination. Whatever the reason, he used the term *citoyen* instead of *monsier* in the letters he wrote to fulfill his commission.

The trouble was between Atakapas and Opeloussas. A certain [Martin] Duralde, a Basque, was a tool of Don Andrés Armesto, secretary of the Spanish government. This Duralde, moreover, was a schemer, an insinuating meddler, and a mortal enemy of his neighbors, the Romans family. He formed a triumvirate with the curé of Atakapas, a man who was considered a very bad subject, and with a certain Bronier, brother of the Bronier of New Orleans. This triumvirate kept the post in constant turmoil. They wrote to the Spanish colonial government denouncing the use of the term *citoyen* by Saint-Julien and accusing Saint-Julien himself of being a disturber of the peace.[22] The government promptly ordered Saint-Julien to be brought here.

Meantime, Saint-Julien was taking a little fresh air with him wife out on his gallery. Suddenly he noticed the muzzle of a gun pointed at his chest, and his first impulse was to push it away. The gun went off and struck his wife. He tried to snatch the gun from the assassin's hand; but during the tussle, another shot went off and grazed his head, setting his hair on fire. He fell, was pounced upon, and left for dead. He recovered. The Spanish government inveighed against Saint-Julien and treated badly M. Le Blanc [de Blanc] and all those suspected of French leanings. M. Le Blanc was removed from his post. In the month of September, Saint-Julien was thrown into one of the city jails and locked up for three days before being questioned. Not overlooking the proceedings previously drawn up against him, which favored his acquittal, the government sent to Atakapas a commissioner who tried to make him guilty of the murder of his wife. There is nothing as atrocious and as heinous as these machinations against an innocent man. The entire post admitted his innocence, but the real assassins had intrigue and gold. What people these folks are! What souls! What judges! What horrors!

When the country had been handed over by the government that was oppressing him, I sought to allow Saint-Julien some respite. No doubt he was the victim of an error—to put things in the most favorable light—of the judiciary. In our government, the executive branch does not possess the right to interfere in judicial affairs, not even to correct them; however, public clamor won out. Never again could such a thing happen. I had the proceedings brought to me. I reread all the acts, signed and certified by [Joseph] Sorel, and I reexamined the affair carefully. I drafted my decree and communicated it to M. [Pierre] Derbigny, the regular interpreter for the Spanish auditor. Derbigny assured me that each court hearing had convinced him more and more of the innocence of the accused. I found myself agreeing perfectly with what he knew, and I read my decree to Clark, who approved it. I rendered justice to the accused and set him free. That same evening, I had a decision drawn up and sent to the city government. They put it into execution without delay. This act of justice seemed to relieve my heart.

December 3

I was not content with having rescued Saint-Julien from his

December 4

tormentors. Duralde had replaced Dublanc as commander, and [Don Pedro] Piernas had been named as military judge. I had the Spanish commissioners give me orders for them. I charged M. Pothier, whom I named French commissioner of the region, with the task; Saint-Domingue had transferred him to me. There he had fulfilled the functions of assistant engineering officer. Since his arrival here, I had been satisfied with him in the several tests through which I put him. In this case, I gave him the task of going over to Opeloussas and Atakapas. He was to return the command of Atakapas to M. Dublanc and the command of Opeloussas to the person whom M. Dublanc would designate; and finally, he was to remain there performing the functions of French commissioner until the colony was transferred to the United States. I authorized him, should it be necessary, to place these two posts under martial law and expel from those districts [the Reverend Bernard] Barrère, the curé of Atakapas—this muddle-headed fellow had been the contriver of all the discord. Poor Dublanc did not dare accept my reestablishing him in his post.[23] He thought he saw the children of the Inquisition raising their heads again—ruining, banishing, and assassinating him.

Sunday—
Solemn mass
That same day, I asked the ecclesiastical superior Hasset [Thomas Hasset, vicar-general of the diocese], to arrange for the celebration of a solemn high mass at which I would be present and at which the "Domine salvam fac Republicam, Domine salvos fac Consules" should be sung, as stipulated in the concordat. He answered that the Spanish clergy intended to follow the Spanish rule, but I would not accept this lame pretext. I insisted, I obtained the mass, and I attended it. Father Koune celebrated it with a deacon and a subdeacon. All the liturgical honors for such an occasion were rendered.

On his part, the Marquis de Casacalvo wanted to repair the wrongs he had done some time previously. He refused, almost in so many words, to allow the intervention of the Spanish authority, which I had called for, against the infractions and outrages of Adjutant Commander Burthe, whom he had endeavored to incite against me. At this time, the marquis dedicated to us (and this time there was no Burthe) a ball on the eighth of December. At least 150 women were present, beautiful in their natural loveliness and finery. There was a blend of Louisiana women—French, American, and Spanish, the last in very great numbers. All of the officers of the Spanish troops were there in uniform. In addition to four masters of ceremonies, M. de Casacalvo himself did the honors with as much attention as grace. At the head of his staff, he came to receive my wife as she descended from her carriage. A box, guarded throughout the night by a grenadier of the Louisiana Regiment, was reserved for her and her company. The *soirée* was divided between a concert and dances. At two o'clock in the morning, an *ambigu* was served in lavish abundance.[24] A dazzling quantity of candles lit up superb decorations. Several blank invitations had been sent to my wife, who did not fill in any of them. We left at eight o'clock in the morning. The marquis left only after we did.

It would not have been French for me to remain in his debt. I returned the courtesy on the sixteenth of December. The harmony of the event was disturbed by a fire that broke out between eight and nine o'clock in the evening. The conflagration began in a house belonging to a free mulatto woman. A wind was blowing from the north quite strongly. Fortunately, a spacious garden separated the house, in that direction, from the other buildings similarly constructed of wood. It was not difficult to confine the source of the fire and to watch carefully the flaming sparks that were falling on the rooftops, covered for the most part by shingles.

Recalling the fires of 1788 and 1794 and the eight million piastres fortes which this burned-up city lost, one can excuse the Louisianians for shuddering when they see flames. It was a heart-breaking spectacle, on leaving my house, to meet fathers of families and women, fleeing tearfully and screaming; or in another section, to see loaded-down slaves, followed by their masters, heading in the general direction of the port, while at the port itself, terrified sailors were cutting loose their cables and allowing their ships to drift away.

Amidst screams and frightful confusion, the French as well

as the Spanish and American languages mingled with one another on all sides. People fell pell-mell over each other into the slush and mud that covered the middle of the road. By the end of an hour, the roof of the house collapsed, and the fire threw off fewer burning cinders.

The Marquis de Casacalvo came running up. The regular troops and fire brigades were bustling about—the former restoring order, the latter cutting communications. As for the militia who were property owners, the greater number of them ran home. But by ten o'clock, sixteen patrols on foot were policing the streets.

Once the fire was under control and almost extinguished, we, that is, the Marquis de Casacalvo and I, came back to rejoin the pleasant company we had left at the house and which since then had greatly increased.

You never saw anything more brilliant. A lovely atmosphere prevailed in all the drawing rooms. Entertainment lasted twelve hours. The guests danced boleros, *gavottes*, English dances, French and English quadrilles, and *galopades*. Eight tables accommodated card players and high-stake gamblers. Twenty oil lamps and 220 wax candles were burned. Sixty places were set at the main table, 24 at the small table, and 146 on 32 small round tables. In addition, hundreds ate standing up here and there. As a local touch, twenty-four gumbos were served, six or eight of which were sea turtle. Throughout the night, a buffet with plenty of Bavarian sweets was served with tea, coffee, chocolate, and consommés. I thus returned to the Spanish commander a social courtesy which has since been admired. The party broke up at eight o'clock in the morning. The officers of the Spanish corvette, the *Desempeño*, postponed their departure and, mooring in front of my house for the night, attended the party. They left at nine-thirty the next morning, after doing credit to our pleasure.

The ball was about to begin the day before when I received from the commissioners of the United States, Claiborne and Wilkinson, a notice dated the seventh of the month to the

effect that, having received at Fort Adams my announcement
that the country had been transferred to me, they were em-
barking with their troops on light barges and coming down
the river.[25] I had not yet left the ball when I was informed that
they were landing at the Mether [James and George Mather]
plantation, about six leagues from the city. I was ready to lay
this pointless burden [the post as colonial prefect] down with
pleasure.

The members of the local government tormented me to
sanction yet one more decree relative to the regulation of the
Negroes. They pointed out that they daily felt an extreme
need for it. They came back to the charge several times. I kept
refusing on the grounds that this was on the eve of my laying
down my ephemeral power. Finally, I gave in. I explained the
motives for my conduct in the preamble of a decree that I
drew up for the purpose. A good deal of trouble was taken to
hasten printing and publication [on December 17, 1803] of
this decree. It will be my testament, in the name of the French
Republic, on behalf of this dear Louisiana. I have also established a fire brigade among the militia, which lacked one.

M. Wadson [Decius Wadsworth], colonel of engineers,
temporary aide-de-camp, and secretary of the United States
commission, notified me officially of the arrival of the commissioners and inquired on December 19, 1803, at what time I
would receive them. I indicated that I would do so from noon
until two o'clock.[26] Twenty-four dragoons in full-dress uniform preceded them, and a nineteen-gun salute welcomed
them.

Claiborne, between thirty and thirty-five years old, was
tall, with a typical American complexion and bearing, a kind
face, and deliberate speech. Both he and Wilkinson wore
shoulder sashes. We agreed that we would follow in general
the forms of procedure observed with the Spaniards. I called
upon them the next day at their camp. My escort comprised
more than 150 people. Many of the residents, officers from
the militia, etc., accompanied me. There is nothing a well-
liked governor might not obtain from these people. We were

received in full military fashion. While we were there, the municipal council arrived in carriages. I introduced its members, then we retired.

*December
20*

*Transfer of
Louisiana
to the
United
States*

The day, which was to be the first of a truly new era for the Mississippi shores, finally dawned. At ten-thirty, I saw myself surrounded at my house by all the municipal officials, the general staff, a great number of officers, and an even greater number of French citizens from all walks of life. With this retinue, I set out on foot toward the city hall.

The day was beautiful and the temperature as balmy as a day in May. Lovely ladies and city dandies graced all the balconies on the Place [d'Armes]. The Spanish officers could be distinguished in the crowd by their plumage. At none of the preceding ceremonies had there been such a throng of curious spectators. The eleven rooms of the city hall were filled with all the beautiful women of the city.

The Anglo-American [American only] troops at last appeared. Captain Costille, assigned to meet them at the [Tchoupitoulas] gate of the city, sent his aide-de-camp Traisnel to notify Major Vinache, the Place [d'Armes] commandant. The latter took my orders and had the troops enter. To the roll of drums they emerged in ranks down along the riverfront at the Place [d'Armes] and, facing the militia, which was standing with its back to the city hall, arranged themselves there in battle formation.

The commissioners Claiborne and Wilkinson were received at the foot of the stairs of the city hall by the major of engineers, Vinache; the commander of the militia, Livaudais; and the secretary of the French commission, Daugerot. I came forward to greet them, halfway across the meeting room. Claiborne seated himself in an armchair on my right and Wilkinson seated himself in another on my left. I announced the purpose of the ceremony. The commissioners presented their powers to me; their secretary read them aloud. Immediately after, I ordered to be read (1) the treaty of transfer, (2) my powers, and (3) the act of exchange of ratifications. Then I declared that I was transferring the country to the United

States, repeating solemnly the terms in which my powers were conceived.

I handed over the keys to the city, tied together with tricolor ribbons, to M. Wilkinson and, immediately afterwards, I absolved from their oath of allegiance to France the inhabitants who chose to remain under the domination of the United States. The minutes were read, first in French by Daugerot, and then in English by Wadsworth. Both sides, together with the respective secretaries, affixed their signatures.

We moved to the main balcony of the city hall. As we appeared, the French colors were lowered and the American flag was raised. When they reached the same level, both banners paused for a moment. A cannon shot was the signal for salvos from the forts and the batteries.

Captain Charpin and his Company of French Citizens had stood at attention since morning as a guard of honor for the French flag. Their sergeant major, Legrand, came forward and received the French flag from the hands of the sublieutenant, Dusseuil, who had lowered it. Legrand draped it around himself like a sash and, escorted by two officers of the company with drawn swords, retired to his position in the middle of the company.

I came down from the balcony with the commissioners of the United States. Arriving midway in front of the troops of the militia, I said to them: "Members of the militia, you have given proof of zealous devotion to the French flag during the short time that it has just flown over these regions. The French Republic will be informed of it. I express my gratitude to you in the name of its government. As of this moment, you pass under the domination of the United States: they are now your sovereign. I turn your command over to their commissioners. Obey them as the representatives of the United States."[27] I joined the flag bearers, and we filed out of the square to the roll of drums.

The memory of that event will never leave me. Above all, what a spectacle it was, both solemn and touching, to see fifty

French citizens brought together there. By diverse paths and hazards and of their own accord, they rallied there, some 2,500 leagues from their native land, to pay homage to the flag of their country! This standard, brought over to those regions for a long duration, this standard that for twelve years had never ceased to march onward and to spread afar the glory of France, was voluntarily withdrawing and retreating back upon Europe.

The company improvised there that day had borne arms in defense of its mother country since the beginning of the Revolution. Its soldiers had bearing and a military clip; they marched with precision, order, dignity, and a touching calm that left a striking impression on the spectators. More than one tear was shed at the moment when the flag disappeared from that shore. We withdrew, passing before the entire line of Anglo-American troops, who presented arms, and the flags and the officers, who saluted us.

Having retired to the reception hall of the prefecture, the soliders deposited the flag. I told them that I would request their temporary commander to give me their names, which I would immediately send on to the First Consul. I concluded by inviting all of them together and each one individually to the festivities of that evening.

The militia officers, wearing the tricolor cockade, rushed in. Showing it to me, they said, "We are still wearing it as we present ourselves to you at this time; it will be eternally dear to us, as well as the memory of your brief sojourn in these regions." There were tears in their eyes. I had steeled myself for the ordeals of this day, but I had not expected that one and consequently was not prepared for it. I mustered what little strength I had left to reply briefly and then fled to my office.

The celebration closed with a dinner and a *soirée* in which all society took part without distinction of Spaniards, Americans, or Frenchmen. We raised a solemn toast to the three nations and saluted them to the deafening noise of the cannons. We had hardly finished drinking coffee and other beverages when the dances began, in which the American women, whose charms we have not yet extolled, took part.

The drawing rooms were taken over by games of *écarté*, *braque*, chess, *bête*, *médiateur*, *bouillotte*, and after supper, *creps* [craps].[28] At one o'clock, supper was served. Twelve American officers, for whom I had asked permission to attend from their commanders, were present. Certainly, the banks of the Mississippi had never before seen any gathering or festivities so splendid and so lively. I could not begin to recount all the gracious remarks passed during those twenty-four hours and the expressions of interest and regret offered to us.

When I considered what I wanted to do and what I accomplished during my reign of twenty days, I was not dissatisfied. I could depart from these shores without fearing the remembrances I would leave behind. I have described fully and with satisfaction the circumstances of this double revolution that would create such marvelous changes in the destinies of a people of French origin in a vast country established and commended to the world by France.

The commissioners of the United States pressed me to release the public buildings which the treaty transferred to them.[29] Except for that one point, they were not authorized to take in the name of their government any effects from our artillery, munitions, barracks, etc. I informed the Marquis de Casacalvo about it.

They questioned me unofficially about the boundaries. On this matter, they held a greatly mistaken idea that they had learned from Washington, where, intentionally or in good faith, the notion prevailed that the boundaries extended as far as Mobile. I corrected them and emphasized that, in any case, I had no orders regarding that point.

I felt rather sure that I could quickly conclude what still remained to be settled with the commissioners. They were most willing to free me from my burden. I had already asked the Spaniards to order the transfer of the posts, which the Marquis de Casacalvo promised to do.[30]

At the end of December the prairies in the American wil-

December
21

derness are set on fire. Flaming clouds, like beautiful sunsets, can be seen at night that time of year to the farthest reaches of the horizon. Such is the cause of this peculiar phenomenon in these regions. The short days of this season end at six-thirty. The river was rising visibly, having reached about 4½ feet, and would continue to swell steadily until March. In spite of the hoary frosts, the thermometer never went below seven or eight degrees Reaumur [45° to 46° F].

Still another ball was held! This one moved me, since the

January
3, 1804

city officials gave it in honor of my wife on the third of January. It was really beautiful, and the women had never been more elegant and fresh-looking in their finery. Four commissioners—Messrs. Boré; the mayor, Fortier; Faurie; and Derbigny—did the honors.

Halfway through the supper, a dove, perched upon a spray of roses, descended in front of my wife, seated at the table. It carried in its beak a note which read:

PORTRAIT OF MADAME LAUSSAT

You see combined in her
Virtues and attractions;
You see the faithful portrait
Of her soul in her features;
Affable, sensible and good,
Virtuous without pride,
And beautiful without vanity;
Everything about her is charming.[31]

We were the last to leave, toward six o'clock in the morning. It was very cold for the country, with abundant rainfall rapidly followed by a violent and icy north wind.

January
8

During the night of the eighth of January, an unfortunate potential for trouble broke out between the French and Anglo-Americans at the regular public ball. Two quadrilles, one French, the other English, formed at the same time. An American, taking offense at something, raised his walking stick at one of the fiddlers. Bedlam ensued. Claiborne remained quiet until Clark roused him. Unable to explain himself in French, Claiborne appeared embarrassed and weak; he yielded at first, then endeavored to reassert his authority.[32] In the end, he resorted to persuasion rather than to rigorous measures in order to silence the American, who was a simple surgeon attached to the troops. The French quadrille resumed. The American interrupted it again with an English quadrille and took his place to dance. Someone cried, "If the women have a drop of French blood in their veins, they will not dance." Within minutes, the hall was completely deserted by the women. The Marquis de Casacalvo, who was present, continued to play cards, laughing up his sleeve. He had gumbo served to two or three women who came to him for protection, and he maliciously played his hand.

Claiborne spoke to me of the incident. "There you have a picture of the feelings that stir up people." I replied, "See to it that they do not clash over things more serious and more important." He retorted, "The people of Louisiana love France dearly; I get proofs of it all the time." There is no doubt that they loved France. It would take the ablest of American statesmen to erase this fond predilection and a great display of kindness on the part of the new government.

The following Sunday there was no ball; but there was one again on the twenty-second of January. *January 22*

Meanwhile, the *Telegraph* of January 11 had published a letter written under the pseudonym "The Philadelphian." It refuted the assertion that at the moment when the French flag had been lowered, everywhere, except for a scattering of applause coming from a group of Americans, tears and sadness were manifest, and it took this opportunity to insult the Company of French Citizens. The printer was immediately summoned to reveal the name of the author. He declared that Relf, an associate of Chew and Relf Company, commonly assumed to be M. Clark's commercial house, had brought it in. They looked up Relf; he denied the letter. Four young men from the Company of French Citizens, together with many of their other comrades, published a militant reply in the next issue of the same newspaper, the *Telegraph* [January 14, 1804]. Clark was apparently the real author, but nobody claimed authorship.

Clark was possessed by restlessness and a craving for domination and distinction. To tell the truth, he really did not know what he wanted. He readily accepted affection and flattery from others, as well as their prejudices and animosities of the most contradictory kind; and he fluctuated between them. Even though he repeatedly said that he did not seek any prominent position, he found it strange that anyone else but he had been charged with the confidence of his government, and he could not disguise his grudge. He bustled around a great deal in order to seem important and, in so doing, often made foolish mistakes. Such was the man who hid behind the pseudonym "The Philadelphian."

January 24 The ball began in a generally bad atmosphere. The city officials had ruled that one should dance successively two rounds of French quadrilles, one round of English quadrilles in groups of twelve partners, and one round of waltzes. This order was being observed, uninterrupted by an English quadrille into which fourteen or fifteen dancers had slipped. However, another group with only twelve partners, one of whom was General Wilkinson, had finished its round. Suddenly protests were raised; immediately, one of the municipal officers charged with keeping order, called out, "French quadrille!" It began and apparently order was restored when all of a sudden, as if planned, remarks and murmurings were heard.

General Wilkinson was then seen, with a friendly look, leading a French citizen by the name of Gauthier toward the guard. The rumor spread that the young man had been arrested. The uproar redoubled. General Wilkinson got up on a bench and interspersed a few words of bad French with his English statements. M. Claiborne got up beside the general. He pointed to an individual, Labalch, a health officer of the 110th Demibrigade [Regiment], just arrived from Saint-Domingue, whom I placed on the brig *Argo*. General Wilkinson asked, "What do you want?" Labalch answered, "That the posted rules be complied with." At these words, the general began to conduct Labalch, as he had Gauthier, to the guardhouse. His release was demanded because he was a

French officer. Labalch was asked for his word of honor, which he gave. "He's only a health officer," someone pointed out. The general exclaimed several times, "Ah! He is a man-killer." Saint-Abit [Saint-Avid] then pledged his word of honor for him. Labalch left. While Saint-Abit was still speaking with the general, a United States officer presented himself to speak to the general. Saint-Abit unintentionally pushed this officer aside with a brusque movement. This was taken as an insult. Thirty Americans and Frenchmen scuffled with each other. The guard of regular troops came in. Saint-Abit escaped death by a miracle. He was unarmed and had been beaten and wounded.

Teihl, who was lodging nearby, arrived armed with his saber, and he spoke to General Wilkinson. M. [Samuel] Davis, followed by several American captains, inquired why that saber at his side. Of violent temper and extraordinary physical strength, Teihl had long commanded a corvette under the French at Saint-Domingue. He was considered Clark's tool and his champion, and he was bound to him by financial interests. Clark had him appointed captain of the port. Teihl stepped away from the general. Lafitte, another Frenchman, joined him. They reproached Davis for having picked the wrong time. The Americans fell on Teihl, who reached a nearby closet, and the quarrel ended. It was because Saint-Abit and Teihl had signed the reply to "The Philadelphian" that they were thus singled out for attacks. The women had left at the beginning of the quarrel. Only twelve or fifteen French ladies stayed on. Other than these, there were only men present. General Wilkinson intoned the "Held [Hail] Columbia," accompanied by the music of his staff, then "God save the King," then huzzas. The French, on their side, sang "Enfants de la Patrie, Peuple français, peuple de frères," and shouted "Vive la Republique!" It was an infernal brawl. After this cabaret scene, Claiborne and Wilkinson, escorted by Americans and the band, returned to their homes.

The young Frenchmen, Gauthier and Lebalch, were cited in court the next day, as a formality only, and then released.

Clark, who served as their interpreter, had not appeared on the night of the ball, although customarily he never missed any of them. He was generally regarded as the instigator of these disorders. Saint-Abit boldly challenged those who had attacked him, but in vain; no one showed up. Teihl manhandled Davis, who managed to escape by offering humble apologies. Finally, the influential and right-minded Americans believed that the best thing to do was to invite the French to a reconciliation banquet. The French had to be coaxed a great deal and finally accepted. So this war of esteem came to an end.

The principal responsibility for the fracas belonged to the American leaders. They played a role in it, encouraged it, participated in it. Claiborne kept repeating, "To bring these folks to their senses, we'll have to aim cannons at them and knock down the walls of the city from top to bottom." Clark, their interpreter, let it be rumored around that "until two or three Frenchmen have been hanged, we will not rule over this country."

The English have dumped the debris from the military hospital of Mole [Santo Domingo] upon us. They loaded it on the *Express* on the seventeenth of September, and the ship moored on the twentieth of January, 1804, at La Balise. It had put in at Santiago. The Americans, displeased at its landing, held it up willy-nilly below Plaquemines. I sent it help and then sent it on with the *Argo* on the twenty-third of February.[33]

February 1 We saw M. Folck, colonel in the Spanish army and commander of Spanish Florida, who was in New Orleans with his two sons. Short and slim like a Catalonian, he was highly successful. The Marquis de Casacalvo both detested and flattered him.

Swallows were flitting about, but the cold was severe. A stiff north wind blew for twenty-four hours; one could hear it whistle through the chinks in the doors and windows. Penetrating to the very marrow of the bone, it made one shiver. This was no longer just one of those gusts of wind that clears the atmosphere. The sky was cloudy and nothing relieved the cold that we were enduring. There was no ice; the barometer [Laussat means thermometer here] was just above freezing inside the house! The Mississippi, after rising and receding for several days, was definitely rising again.

Finally on March 6, 1804, the northwesterly wind brought us right back into the heart of winter. This time, we had ice cream, superbly made by my chef right at the very gate to the tropics. The storm reminded me of the equinoctial tempest that we weathered just a year before near La Balise, when we lost twelve days in tacking. And yet, in 1804, the flood stage came two months later than the year before, as would the low water. At the same time, we reached the last days of March and the first days of spring. The fruit trees were covered with blossoms. The orange grove was redolent. It adorned our yard in three long lanes and perfumed the air. The atmosphere was intoxicating. I recall having read that the forests of Senegal are likewise covered with fragrant trees, which, at first, affect the senses delightfully and soon thereafter cause a fever. These delights are the cause of one of the unbearable inconveniences of such sojourns, and the gardens of Armide [heroine whose enchanted garden led men to forget war in favor of love, from Torquato Tasso's sixteenth century work, *Gerusalemme liberata*] are enchanting only in fables. Birds warbled everywhere and the harmonious and varied song of the lovely mockingbird resounded near the houses.

March 6

March 31

The sunrises and sunsets resumed their rich robes. The blue in the sky was gorgeous, whether in the burst of sunrise, at the decline of day, in the brilliant clearness of the stars, or in the soft glow of the moon. There were no mosquitoes or snakes yet. The grass was sprouting vigorously and forming a green carpet—a refreshing scene on both banks of the Mississippi. The river did not carry any silt, become muddy, or overflow. It looked like a vast moving carpet that rolled majestically beneath our windows. Navigators ascended and descended it in rows of barges, flatboats, lightboats, and pirogues, loaded with products from the factories of Europe and the fields of Louisiana. An enchanting picture, the magnificent springtime in this country!

The day before, at noon, I had ridden on horseback as far as the bayou [Saint John]. I liked riding there. The bayou contrasts with the banks of the river by its own well-defined banks and its narrow bed meandering from its harbor. It contrasts with the fields of the river by its group of pretty houses, its scenic harbor, and that array of small sailboats and covered boats which handle the commerce from the lakes.

I had brought to this country an extensive library. Being sent to Martinique, I could not, in wartime, take my library there. I wanted to keep only a small part of it. A good number of books were easily given away, mostly the classics and some current works; the local people do not care for the sciences. I was busy at that time sorting out those which I meant to keep. One after another, I sold several of the dearest and most faithful companions of my life; it broke my heart to part with them. One lot deserted me on March 31: Montaigne— the very copy I purchased when I was nineteen and I have read and reread since; J.-J. Rousseau—a small eighteen- volume set, which accompanied me on my promenades and in my travels; Montesquieu—eight volumes of twelve, in which I read and reread the *Décadence des Romains*, *L'Esprit des lois*, *Le Temple de Gnide*, and *Le Dialogue de Scilla*; my Corneille and my Racine, which were daily reading; and so on, and so on. They had been the witnesses and the confidants of my early studies. I bought them myself. They had gone to Béarn; they had accompanied me to Paris—to the rue du Petit- Reposoir, rue Notre-Dame-des-Victoires, rue Caumartin, rue de la Sourdière, rue Daguesseau, and the rue Neuve-des- Capucins. There was no memory, no joy, no sorrow in my life in which they had not played some part. They had followed my fate, and one of its strange aspects was that I had come to the banks of the Mississippi to separate from them. It was done! I would never see them again.

On the twenty-seventh of March, 1804, the commissioners of the United States placed in my hands a protest expressed in the following terms:

The undersigned commissioners of the United States, appointed to take possession of the Province of Louisiana, have noted in your letters of the 21 and 25 January (30 nivôse and 4 pluviôse) last, that you speak of Spain's retaining possession of West Florida.

It is not the intention of the undersigned to investigate the right of Spain to that tract, or to state opinions with respect to the limits of the ceded territory; but solemnly to protest that nothing done on their part, shall be construed as a relinquishment of the claims of the United States, *to the Colony or Province of Louisiana, with the same extent which it had actually in the hands of Spain (on 1 day of October 1800, the date of the Treaty of San Ildefonso), and which it had when France possessed it and such as it ought to be after the Treaties subsequently entered into between Spain and other states.*

Accept assurances of our high and respectful esteem.[34]

I passed this document on to the Marquis de Casacalvo through M. Armesto, whom he had sent to me.

The enterprising spirit of the United States was already showing itself in Louisiana. Traders were going up the Missory [sic], some traveling all over the Louisiana Territory. They wagered openly that they would have an open port on the Pacific Ocean within five years, and their commissioners in New Orleans cast covetous glances toward the Floridas! Before long, the United States will give Spain trouble; the acquisition of Louisiana has increased their ambition. *March 27*

I have several times praised in passing the character of the Louisianians. I have no intention of taking back what I have said; but I should discuss the subject in some detail. The healthy thing about this country was the farmer, whether he was landowner or sharecropper. He was sober; thrifty; regular in his habits; hardworking; and even parsimonious, a trait which, in a newly born country, was preferable to prodigality. The houses, the furnishings, and the surroundings of a rich man worth eighteen, twenty, or thirty thousand piastres fortes were the same as those of the man who had less than a thousand piastres fortes of income. The personal property of Madame Almonaster, who owned at the time no less than 200,000 francs in rental and capital assets, was not worth 5,000 francs in all. *April*

Character of the Louisianians

The Louisianian was extremely vainglorious of his numerous family connections; he had an endless line of cousins. Yet for all that, Louisianians were not overly eager to look up one another, and they remembered their genealogy only at weddings and funerals. Their pride of race and origin went far back; yet the colony there, founded a short time before, did not date back beyond 1700 in Mobile. When they quoted people, I did not find it necessary to go back even fifty years to find a father or grandfather who was a simple officer of the navy, or a soldier or a clerk or even a shoemaker who had come with the first group of settlers from France. The exceptions applied to a few rare principal lineages among the upper classes.

Proud of this country, which he praised to the skies, the Creole also cherished France. He never mentioned O'Reilly without hate and horror, and he despised the Spanish government, whose depravity he related at length. Yet, he showed an even greater antipathy toward the Americans. On the other hand, devoid of energy, organization, and public spirit, he would allow himself to be subjugated without complaining, except when beside his fireplace or while strolling up and down his galleries.

Louisianians preserved the spirit of adventure from their forebears and were enterprising in their efforts to amass a fortune. They bought and sold on long-term credit—a practice that derived from that custom of arriving and starting with nothing, prospering, and facing up to debts contracted on one's word alone. From this practice derived also their general laxity in keeping engagements, while maintaining an admirable tolerance in conceding to others delay after delay.

The Americans, in contrast, introduced the strictness of their laws and exactness of their customs. For two months they had been apprehending and imprisoning debtors. The Louisianians found this unbearable, and everything was in confusion. Their leaders were blind enough not to grasp the unwise policy of so swift a change; however, it was hopeless. The poor Louisianians would just have to adjust.

The customs of the city differed strangely from those of the country. The city resident was often reckless; the man who lived there without incurring huge debts was rare. I was thinking of him especially when I spoke of the uncertainty of payments.

The women were drowned in luxury. Inside and out, they were glutted with superfluous things, but often lacked necessities. They had taste, elegance, coquetry, and a precocious frivolity; but they could not be counted on either for intellectual resources or for conversational charm. Generally, there prevailed a great deal of idle gossip in their society. They knew even the shadiest stories about other women and kept the secret badly. Some mothers of families were good managers; however, most of them were noted for the indolence which seemed to constitute the dominant tendency in their character.

Nowhere as in the city were there so many single women. The burdens of family life frightened men. The mulatto women were in great demand and were much cheaper. Even one kept at great expense had no qualms of conscience about her infidelity to the lover she ruined or betrayed.

The young men married without fortune. The parents did not dispossess themselves, and the young men spent their best years thus and became sottish. *April*

A recent work brought from France by M. Picot [James Pitot] caused a considerable stir. The book was titled *Vue de la Colonie Espagnole du Mississippi ou des provinces de la Louisiane et les Florides Occidentales en 1802, par un observateur résident sur les lieux* (par Berquin-Duvallon, rue Saint-Bénôit, nombre 21— 1803). The author, [Pierre-Louis] Berquin, was the king's procurator at Saint-Domingue before the Revolution, and he had married there. At the time of the fire at the Cape, he fled to Baltimore. From there he took to New Orleans the remnants of his fortune, including some very bad Negroes, who were jailed almost immediately. The governor and the auditor quietly returned the Negroes to Berquin, a few at a time. He spent 2½ years here and then picked up and left in the spring of 1802. *Berquin's work on Louisiana*

He described the colony in bilious colors. His work was filled with sarcasm. He saw nothing but marshland and reptiles. In the men he sought only their defects; in the women, *Portrait of the auditor, Vidal* only the ridiculous. He had a narrow and warped mind. His best chapter was the one on the judiciary and on the auditor, "Don Maria-Nicolas Vidal-Chavez-Etcheverry de Madrigal y Valdez, teniente governador civil y auditor de guerra de los Principes de la Luisiana y de la Florida Occidental, Juez," etc. Vidal's name alone is an epigram, and it must be admitted that, after all, the subject is rich. There was not a more diseased heart, a more twisted mind, a more mealymouthed disposition hidden behind a yellow countenance shaded by black. And yet, in difficult matters of government, Vidal was a mastermind. The Marquis de Casacalvo consulted him when it came to making a decision between Burthe and me.

Let the poor devil rest in peace. Let us simply add that he had as his mistress a foul-smelling mulatto, an important channel through whom all favors flowed. His weakness for African blood was displayed on festival days; his doorstep was a gathering place for Negro dancing. He had two splendid Negro males. In the wintertime, instead of using a warming pan in his bed, he had them get into the bed first to warm it up, and then he would get in between them. Sometimes they rebuked him. On one such occasion, when one of those hefty fellows seemed to want to pounce upon him, he fell to his knees and cried out, "For God's sake, don't kill me, for I am in the state of mortal sin" ("Por Dios, no me mates: que estoy en pecado mortal").

American commanding general   I would call this man Vidal the personification of the Spanish spirit in this country, just as I would call Wilkinson the quintesscence of American generals. Imagine a general with three to four thousand troops scattered across an area of hundreds of thousands of leagues, fluttering back and forth from morning until night, pretending to be Turenne and Washington, and acting the important military chief toward a thousand fairly well-trained, scattered soldiers in a large place, *rari nantes* [Laussat quotes incompletely from Virgil's *Aeneid* (book 1, line 118): *rari nantes in gurgite vasto* or "a few swimmers in a vast sea"]. The Americans made a great to-do over the posting of five or six sentinels. A cannon was fired morning and evening, soldiers were made to run the gauntlet once a day, and, finally, the band was made to play mess call at the barracks. The rest of the day, the band played at the government building, where the members of the commission and their retinue lived it up riotously, each man paying his share. They smoked noisily from dusk until ten o'clock at night, and people passing by stopped to listen.

The Americans were swarming in from the northern states. Each one turned over in his mind a little plan of speculation, that is to say, of Jewry; they were invading Louisiana as the holy tribes invaded the land of Canaan. Their tendency, and a sort of instinct, is to exclude from these privileged regions any generation but their own. Nature is more powerful, and they shall fail before the general rush by the nations.

Americans invading the country

My preparations for departure were progressing. I hurried Vinache with the official reports, Molier with arsenal reports, and Navailles with the financial reports. I called in some assistance, for it was no easy task to close all the branches of a fourteen-month administration. But I finally reached the end.

Spanish and French preparations to leave Louisiana

The Spanish commissioners had informed me that they would soon evacuate their troops, who finally left on April 11, 1804, aboard a large ship loaded with artillery. The parting and the farewells were touching. As far as the eye could see, soldiers and officers lined up on the deck, even on the highest yardarms. They returned to Pensacola. The keys to the barracks they had occupied were thereupon turned over to Vinache and Costille, who immediately handed them over to Wadsworth and Watkins, agents of the United States commissioners. The magazines were also released. I could now leave the battlefield.

April 20

I had neglected nothing during my mission which I believed serviceable to my country.[35] In this respect, I should make a cursory note of the information I have collected on Bay del Carmen. Honoré Fortier had just come from there, where he had still found several French families. This area blocks the entrance to a bay that bears its name on the western corner of the Yucatan Peninsula, between the eighteenth and nineteenth degree of north latitude, ninety-third and ninety-fourth degree of longitude from the meridian of Paris,

Bay del Carmen at the Yucatan Peninsula, formerly frequented advantageously by the French

in the south of the Gulf of Mexico. A small craft can enter
through the entrance at Puerto Réal, which has no more than
six or seven feet of water; and a ship enters by the Jicalango
entrance, where there is a treacherous bar and from twelve to
twenty Spanish *palmes* [ancient unit of measure equal to
either the width or length of the human palm] of water.

The bay is surrounded by lagoons and the mouths of rivers.
The river containing the most logwood is the East River (Rio
del Este); the lagoon containing the most logwood is the Pan-
chaca. They cut the timber and within three years the cuttings
regenerate themselves. Timber is most abundant there. The
best and greatest quantities of logwood come from this bay.
Foreigners are not permitted to enter. The wood is gathered
at Campêche, where Spanish ships pick it up. The French
were admitted in 1780 to buy the wood at the Isla del Carmen
under their own flag. They took advantage of the occasion to
develop a lucrative illegal trade with Guatemala. It was then
that some French people settled there, where some still remain. The city has a garrison of 4,500 persons.

On the twelfth of March, I began to pay my farewell visits,
accompanied by my faithful Charpin, who took me
everywhere. One day I had dinner at M. Boré's home in the
country. I made my round of the bayou, where civilities and
attentions had been showered upon me. I wanted to acknowledge the thousands of kindnesses that we had received
from both men and women. After that, I went to see the
heads of the Spanish staff. Last of all, I called on the Marquis
de Casacalvo, who was in the midst of several attendants. He
had assembled those who were in some way attached to the
crown of Spain because of favors, pensions, or appointments.
He had prepared a state reception. He received me at the
head of the stairs, after sending three others to meet me at the
gate, and he accompanied me himself as far as the street. A
half hour later, he returned the visit and I followed the same
protocol, point by point.

I announced myself to the commissioners of the United
States and fulfilled the same diplomatic obligation with the
same formality. "Having been entrusted," I told them, "with

*Farwell
visits*

a public responsibility by my country to yours on so memorable an occasion, I come today, in the name of the people of France to greet the people of America in the persons of their commissioners. I consider myself singularly privileged to have participated in this event, because to Louisiana, so dear to France, it will no doubt bring happiness, and to our respective nations, further reasons for mutual affection. I like to think that similar sentiments fill the hearts not only of the present members of the United States government, but of each of its citizens." General Wilkinson replied that they would inform their government of my actions on this occasion and of the manifest feeling with which I accompanied them. M. Claiborne, on his part, assured me that he shared my hopes and did not doubt that the French government would cooperate with the American.

Half an hour later, I received a return visit from the American commissioners, who were accompanied by a brilliant retinue. They extended kind wishes for my happiness and that of my family. I took this opportunity to commend my family to them for the rest of their stay. They accepted this commission very politely.

That was my last official act in Louisiana. After that, I saw the municipal council again and received Bellechasse, who was in command of some officers of the militia in uniform. I will say no more of the country; it is too painful to have known it and then to have been separated from it. [36]

I had arranged secretly with the American vessel *Natchez* to go to Martinique at the end of March. I followed the progress of its repairs and equipping. Often during that last month I would look toward it. Like Calypso, I listened to the blows of the ax; I watched as it prepared gradually to hoist its sails. The ship was loaded. Since fate intended me to take this new risk, I would require no other mentor to cast me into the sea. My daughters wanted to know where the little brig was that I was supposed to take and were most excited when they finally discovered it. Even so, it was imperative that one morning the vessel should slip away unnoticed.

While I was chatting with my family in my study, I caught

Chartering of the Natchez to take me to Martinique

sight of the vessel moving away from the shore. I offhandedly closed my shutters. The ship moved rapidly and went to wait for me about two leagues below the city, at the Batture des Religieuses.

The following day, April 21, 1804, at five o'clock—at sunrise—I sank back in the carriage that the intendant Morales kindly loaned me and arrived with my traveling companions across from the Laronde plantation, where the *Natchez* was moored.[37] The gale that had been blowing for the past twenty-four hours ripped an anchor loose, and someone had gone to the city to get another.

At last we ran eight tacks before rounding the English Turn; we were off to a good start. Our crew was composed of one American captain, Songy; one first mate; four sailors; one cook; and one cabin boy. The passengers with me were an administrative officer, a secretary, and my chief steward.

I took a long time getting settled, so desirous was I to take my mind off the whole affair. On the first night, we dropped anchor in front of Plaquemines.

April 21

On Monday we came to the anchorage of La Balise to spend the night. By eight o'clock the next day we had crossed the bar and were plowing ahead. After that we kept to the open sea.

I leave the Mississippi River

From then on we had beautiful weather. The waves moved just enough to enliven the view. The waters changed their colors that Wednesday. I read and walked the deck, from which I looked at the empty spaces.

Tuesday, May 1

We skirted the Bahama Channel, saw the island of Cuba, the city of Havana, and, on the other side, the Floridas. This meetingplace of navigators is famous for its shipwrecks. "There isn't a week," said our English pilot, "in which one does not take place." It would be useless to try to figure out its rules. There are sometimes violent currents that carry a ship off course without its even knowing it; and there are strong north and northeast winds along the coast of Cuba. The best thing to do is let oneself go without thinking about it. The residents of Providence are allowed to fish all year and to cut lumber in this area, on their pledge to assist ship-

Havana and the Bahama Channel

wrecked vessels and their promise not to pillage them. Turtles abound here. We saw one and, not far from it, a large shark. On Monday the sighting placed us at 28°36' latitude, meaning, to our great satisfaction, that we had passed the Martyrs. We turned east at the Cape and moved straight ahead.

We celebrated the First of May, as they always did in my country, like typical sailors, with a *croûte frotée d'ail et de lard.* [38] We could not have been better off had we been with Béarnais in the heart of our mountains.

The Bermudas is a reef that has often deceived navigators. Even today, the French navigation chart places them at 32°20' latitude, 63°32' longitude. In fact, they are really, according to the English chart, at 31°20' latitude, 64°48' longitude; and, as the Bermudas belongs to the English, the presumption is in their favor. I am speaking here of the latitude only. *May 11—* *The Bermudas*

We had the worst kind of weather here at the Cape on Monday and Tuesday, without letup and with a great deal of turbulence and very little progress. Torrents of rain flooded and soaked everything. I wondered what to do to while the time away. I read and reread. Thus I read *The History of the Diet of Westphalia,* and I relearned my Horace, my Virgil, my Corneille, my Racine, and others that I will soon forget again. *Ten days of* *bad weather* *Tuesday,* *May 15*

Then too, I dreamed; I compared the degrees of latitude under which I passed with those under which I have lived for so long, at the 30°, 43°, 49°, and so on. I built castles in the air, made wise plans and foolish ones and speculations for prosperity and for retirement. Time rolled on. Often I calculated the time when I left and when I would arrive at Martinique. Ah, human destiny! I leafed through my volume of Montaigne, as was my commendable habit; I happened to open it to a charming passage in his chapter "On Glory," which read, "The ancient mariner spoke thus to Neptune, in a great tempest: 'Oh, God! Thou mayest save me if thou wilt; and if thou wilt, Thou mayest destroy me. But, whatever, I will always steer my rudder straight.'"

Seafarers in these parts are equally afraid of having a wind and of not having one; storms, calms, and fog contend with one another. During our hours of calm, I admired the im- *May 15* *Calms* mense quantity of living creatures that populate the ocean. They swim through the waves in all directions, and they have an infinite variety of shapes. Sometimes one would take them to be inanimate masses of matter, sometimes plants. So that none of the three kingdoms are missing in the vast expanse of the sea, the floating seaweed, commonly known as *goamon* or *raisin des tropiques*, spawns, grows, propagates itself, and floats over the entire surface, serving as a resting pad and apparently as nourishment for crabs and a host of other microscopic creatures. We have gone over banks of it that looked like islands carried along by the waves.

For a few days, the sun was warm enough to rehearse clearing the decks and to shift the stowage. American navigators call these seas the horse latitudes because they are at times becalmed in these waters, thus having to cast overboard a part of their cargo of horses. We crossed the Tropic of Cancer.

June 4—Crossing the Tropic of Cancer

We were enjoying the sight of birds, harbingers of land, when an English frigate came upon us and fired her guns at us. We hove to. An officer came aboard at seven in the evening to inspect us. I did not see him, thanks to the darkness of the night, which permitted me to remain outside while he was inside, and to stay inside while he was outside. Our captain told him that he was trying to reach the market of Guadeloupe. If his commanding officer permitted us to continue on our way, the officer would raise a torch and then lower it quickly. The signal allowed us to continue our voyage. One day's journey and a tropical sea brought us, about noon, to Point-à-Pitre on Guadeloupe.

Encounter with an English frigate

Shortly thereafter, I went to Basse-Pointe by sea. I went to greet the governor, General Ernouf, and to have a word with him about the state of affairs in Martinique, which was tightly blockaded. I asked for a skilled pilot, a request that he granted at nightfall. I returned to Pointe-à-Pitre overland on horseback. What a terrible day! In blazing sun and scorching climate, I traveled across two fermenting plains of sugarcane, whose offensive smell stifled me. In eighteen hours, I finally arrived at the plantation of M. de Nesles at Petit-Bourg,

Guadeloupe

Experienced pilot

June 6

exhausted. The first thing I did was to stretch out in a hammock and sleep for two hours; still I was glad to have crossed this smiling and prosperous colony. The same evening, after dinner, I continued my trip by boat, and I returned on board ship by dusk. It was six in the evening of the next day before I finally had my pilot on board ship. We quickly raised anchor.

At daybreak on Tuesday, the eighth of this month, we skirted Marie-Galante in heavy weather. On Tuesday, we found ourselves along Dominique. We took in sail for fear of moving ahead too swiftly. A brisk northeaster was blowing, and the sea was surging. We had spent the night worn-out from continuous alerts. We had no end of difficulty in slowing down our speed. Never did a day seem so long; one longed for night. At last we ventured into the Channel of Dominique. All of a sudden, the captain cried out, "Frigate upon us!" It was headed straight at us, full sail, its banner flying high. We immediately hoisted ours in response and, on the advice of the coast pilot, we headed boldly toward her. She took us at our word and, lowering her colors, continued on her way to Dominique. Already we were moaning, "We were touching it, our Martinique! We were looking at it! We had come two thousand leagues! Our course was finished yet was slipping away from us!" We kept looking at it, not believing our eyes.

Finally, it became dark and we headed directly toward land. The breeze was from the east and northeast, and the sea was swelling; no matter, we approached the end of our voyage and were in high spirits.

Between ten and eleven o'clock, despite the darkness, we thought we were able to distinguish some lighted torches off in the distance. We landed at Macouba [a town of about 1,800 inhabitants on the northern tip of Martinique]. We moved along its shores in the thickness of night, drawing toward the rocks of Perle. A few minutes later they hailed us from Anse à Seron. "Send out a boat," someone shouted. Our second and third mates went ashore here. We waited for more than an hour. What fits of impatience! The guards instructed us to hug the coast. Enemy sails were cruising back and forth

June 10

At the moment of arrival, an English frigate was upon us

Our good spirit asserts itself

June 10

Ashore at Prêcher

vigilantly. I made up my mind and asked to go ashore. We were at Bourg du Prêcher. I got into a dinghy with the coast pilot and two sailors. We had hardly started toward land when we caught sight of a brig that was watching our vessel and was moving over. Apparently it was too close to land, for it was not until five in the morning that the little brig, having continued its tacking against the wind, reached the anchorage of Sainte-Pierre. As for me, I missed my leap; a sailor took me on his shoulders [Laussat was five feet one inch in height] and set me down on the shore.

Not far from me, at the top of a hill, I noticed a house through the darkness. I went to it and found some Negroes asleep on benches. I roused them and learned that I was at M. Audibert's residence. They called him; from his window above, he sent me off to the commander of Clermont.

I hurried there, where I was subjected to questioning. The commander provided me with a horse, gave me two footmen, perched me atop the old remains of an English saddle, and sent me, escorted by a couple of sentinels, two leagues farther to the commander of Saint-Pierre, M. Lebertre, major of the battalion. It was pouring buckets of rain. I proceeded along the shore. It was very dark, so I decided to turn over my reins to one of the guides, who led me by them as he wished.

I arrived at Saint-Pierre

At five o'clock, I arrived soaked to the bone at the home of Commander Lebertre. He wanted to know my name; then, without waiting a moment, he wanted me to give him the letters I was carrying. He struck me as a very extraordinary man. I felt riled. Moreover, it seemed to me that such a first appearance in the colony was not at all in good form. I yielded and wrote a letter to the captain general in which I inserted the one I was charged to give him.

At the same time, I left with the commander the letter that I was bringing for the prefect. After that, there I was, tramping up and down the town looking for a place to stay. I finally found one at an inn, where I was given a room on the first floor. But I had the inspiration to go out to the roadstead to see whether my brig was in sight. I found it in place. I called out and rowed out to it. M. Bertin, the prefect, had already received my letter and immediately invited me to come to his house. I accepted.

I have given step by step the details of my stay in Louisiana.[39] It was a great period for the country. I assisted in, and cooperated in, its act of emancipation. I took pleasure in considering everything, setting down minutely even the least circumstances and delineating distinctly Louisiana's last relations with France, which I alone represented. And, finally, I described the departure by our colony for the American Confederation.

End of the Louisiana Memoirs

Notes

BOOK ONE

1 At this time Napoleon Bonaparte was First Consul, not emperor, of France. In 1804, however, he did take the title of Napoleon I, hence the error on Laussat's part is understandable in view of his long service under the emperor. Laussat recalled the circumstances surrounding his appointment as colonial prefect for Louisiana as follows:

> Preoccupied as I was with a desire for a change of place, a sudden inspiration moved my plans in that direction. Almost at the same time, I understood that there was a question of appointing Bernadotte as governor. We knew each other; we were both Béarnais; and his loyal character and noble mind suited me perfectly. Even his faults did not frighten me. He had received me with honor and interest on different occasions. I began to collect books on Louisiana. I devoured them. I filled my mind with this reading and then went to Bernadotte to lay my plans before him. He approved them and informed me that the tribunate had already thought about it. He passed on to me his memoirs, manuscripts, and charts. I wrote four lines on a small-sized sheet of paper saying simply: "I request the First Consul to grant me the colonial prefecture of Louisiana," and I delivered it into his own hands during one of the biweekly audiences which he held with the tribunes.
> "Who told you that I might need a prefect for Louisiana?"
> "The Frankfurt *Gazette.*"
> "The Frankfurt *Gazette* does not know what it is talking about."
> He kept my petition. Two months later, after another such assembly meeting:
> "Well, are you still determined to go to Louisiana? Is it a decision made with sufficient deliberation, and are you set on it?"
> "Yes, sir. I have not taken such a step lightly."
> "Since you do wish it, you shall go to Louisiana."
> August [20], 1802—After a few days, I received my official nomination as colonial prefect from the minister of the French navy.

Pierre Clément de Laussat Journal (from the personal papers of Antoine du Pré de Saint-Maur in Pau, France), Pt. I, Bk. II, 1756–1802, pp. 177–78. The official document for the appointment above is among the Laussat Papers in the Historic New Orleans Collection archives. See also Robert D. Bush, "Documents on the Louisiana Purchase: The Laussat Papers," *Louisiana History,* XVIII (Winter, 1977), 104–107.

2 The 27th Regiment first assigned to the Louisiana expedition was replaced, because of the great number of sick personnel, by the 7th and 5th Infantry Regiments and the 7th Regiment of Dismounted Artillery,

whose general was Claude Victor-Perrin (1764-1841). He had been a comrade in arms to Bonaparte at Toulon (1793), Mondovi (1796), and then at Marengo (1800). He earned promotion to the rank of marshal following his exploits at the Battle of Friedland (1807) and, like Laussat, later served the restored Bourbon monarch, Louis XVIII. Because Bernadotte balked and made so many "exigences," Bonaparte replaced him as captain general of the Louisiana expedition with Victor, after considering several alternatives. On June 4, 1802, Bonaparte wrote to Admiral Denis Decrès, minister of the navy and colonies:

> My intention is that we take possession of Louisiana with the shortest possible delay, that this expedition be organized in the greatest secrecy, and that it have the appearance of being directed toward Saint-Domingue. The troops that I intend for it being on the *Scheldt*, I should like them to depart from Antwerp or Flushing. Finally, I would like for you to let me know the number of men you think should be sent, both infantry and artillery, and for you to present me with a project of organization for this colony— for the army as well as for the civil authority—and for the fortifications and batteries we should have to construct there in order to have a roadstead and some men-of-war sheltered from superior forces. In this regard, I should like you to have made for me a map of the coast from St. Augustine and Florida to Mexico and also a geographical description of the different cantons of Louisiana with the population and resources of each canton.

Correspondance de Napoleon 1ᵉʳ (32 vols.; Paris, 1858–1870), VI, 617–18.
The Louisiana expedition constituted a sizable flotilla of a dozen ships and over three thousand men. For more details on the expedition see Correspondance Général, Colonies—Louisiane in Archives nationales de la marine á Paris, Ser. C13A, vols. 51–52, hereinafter cited as Archives nationales. See also several letters and reports among the Victor Papers in the Historic New Orleans Collection archives; Ronald D. Smith, "Napoleon and Louisiana: Failure of the Proposed Expedition to Occupy and Defend Louisiana, 1801–1803," *Louisiana History*, XII (Winter, 1971), 21–40; E. Wilson Lyon, *Bonaparte's Proposed Louisiana Expedition* (Chicago, 1934); Georges Oudard, *Vieille Amérique: la Louisiane au temps des français* (Paris, 1931); and, Marc de Villiers du Terrage, *Les Dernières Années de la Louisiane française* (Paris, 1903).
3 Impatient with the slowness of preparations, and fearing to arouse suspicion by sending a large flotilla across the Atlantic, Bonaparte ordered an advance party, under the leadership of Laussat, to precede the main force. Laussat, with his family and the advance party, departed aboard the vessel *Surveillant* on January 10, 1803. See instructions to Laussat from Denis Decrès, 16 frimaire an XI (December 7, 1802), in the Laussat Papers.
After having visited the ship docked in the harbor at Rochelle, Laussat observed: "The ship is not as beautiful as the *Republic*, which does honor to this port. I hope, at least, that after having served our apprenticeship on this brig, which is so small, uncomfortable, and filthy, I will be declared a real sailor and my wife a veritable Amphitrite. And so we depart, still happy if, as they flatter me, the newly assigned commander, Girardeau, captain of the frigate, should offer us his cabin." In Villiers, *Louisiane française*, 395.

4   Heavy ice due to a severe winter was the immediate reason for the delay, and the harsh winter continued to hold the flotilla at bay. A second more tragic storm destroyed several ships and damaged others in the spring of 1803. The constant delays, low morale among the troops, increasing costs, weather conditions, and political considerations in Europe—all had their effect upon Bonaparte. The result was the sale of Louisiana to the United States by France, concluded in the treaty of April 30, 1803.

5   Of his departure for Louisiana, Laussat wrote in part:

> At one o'clock in the morning, we were in the Basque harbor. A ship was towed in. It was ours. The *Surveillant* had left at two o'clock in the afternoon for the roadstead of the Île d'Aix. There was a good deal of grumbling everywhere. Alas! More than ever, the wind was quite strong. At daybreak, we put out to sea and at seven-fifteen we boarded the brig. Unfortunately, we missed the hawser that was thrown to us. The wind was blowing fiercely and the sea was surging. Once the brig was leeward, it was impossible for us to approach it. The longboat of the brig having come by just at that moment, my wife, my daughters, Franchon, Adjutant Burthe, and I flung ourselves into it with considerable difficulty. We reached the brig, properly shaken and drenched in this our apprenticeship. So there we were on this ship upon which a new order of things began for us. The wind was favorable. The captain wanted to raise anchor at noon. The schooner had so much trouble in approaching us that we had to approach it instead; we weighed anchor and dropped it again.

Journal, 43–44.

6   Georges Oudard writes, "This former member of the Council of Five Hundred and the tribunate was a man of thirty-six years—intelligent, grandiloquent, honest, and somewhat naive—who began his colonial career with this post. He had never yet left *terra firma*, nor, to judge his reflections, did it seem that he had ever seen a ship before reaching La Rochelle." In *Vieille Amérique*, 264. See also Robert D. Bush, "Colonial Administration in French Louisiana: The Napoleonic Episode, 1802–1803," *Publications of the Louisiana Historical Society*, 2nd ser., II (1975), 36–59.

7   The subject of military and civilian personnel for the Louisiana expedition is well detailed in the correspondence of Laussat with Decrès and Victor. See especially the report of 17 frimaire an XI (December 9, 1802), in the Laussat Papers; see also the Victor Papers.

8   The command was originally assigned to Jouet from Lorient, but he became ill with gout and died a short time later. Girardais was appointed to replace him as captain of the *Surveillant*, a small brig measuring eighty-four feet long by twenty-six feet at her gunwales. The flag was still at half-mast the day Laussat came aboard for the first time. His first impressions of it were anything but encouraging: "When I saw that tiny room into which one must descend by means of a ladder . . . where they had put my wife and myself, and I did not now know where they were going to put my daughters, my heart sank, I assure you. Everything is so dirty in such a small ship. The odor of it is disgusting, and to the eighty men already present, we were going to add, little by little, still another twenty to twenty-five occupants. But one gets accustomed to it, and by the end of the hour that I spent there, I was already used to the idea to

such a point that I did not mind it too much." Journal, 19–20. Overcrowded conditions meant that Laussat had to leave several of his trunks behind.

9 Santander is a port town on the northern coast of Spain. Laussat received his final instructions there. Upon landing, he learned that the marquis de Someruelos was captain general of Cuba and adjacent territories, of which Louisiana was only one, and not the governor of Louisiana. The king of Spain directed orders for the evacuation of the colony to Someruelos. The governor resident in Louisiana was Brigadier General Don Manuel de Salcedo, a man long overdue for retirement and quite infirm. He was under the orders of Someruelos, but the court in Spain dealt only with Louisiana through the latter. Consequently, any orders concerning the colony would have to come from him, not Salcedo. Thus from the outset, Laussat found himself in an awkward political situation in that he was supposed to present his credentials to Someruelos in order to assume responsibility for the colony on behalf of the French government. Laussat explained his embarrassing position in a lengthy letter addressed to Denis Decrès, in Archives nationales, Ser. C13A, vol. 52, 69.

10 Laussat here refers to himself, Girardais, two ensigns, Hurte, Sare, and an aide-de-camp, Ornana.

11 The captain, not the petty officer, noticed that the boat was taking in water. Journal, 49.

12 A *tertulia* is an afternoon tea or social gathering.

13 A treaty was concluded by Napoleon Bonaparte and Pope Pius VII to regulate relations between the Gallican Church and Rome on July 16,1801. It temporarily settled several of the points at issue between the Catholic Church in France and the Vatican.

14 Laussat had been assured that the loading would take only a day, but it actually took five days to count the money. See Archives nationales, Ser. C13A, vol. 52, 69, 76–77. The printed edition of the *Mémoires* gives a slight variation from the handwritten version. See Pierre Clément de Laussat, *Mémoires sur ma vie á mon fils* (Pau, France, 1831), Pt. II, Bk. I, 13.

15 Laussat refers here to the mountain of Thessaly near Ossa. When, according to classical literature, the Titans revolted against Zeus for wishing to reach the sky, they piled Mount Pelion atop Mount Ossa.

16 Negro slaves of Santo Domingo broke into revolt against French rulers during the 1790s. The ferocity of the rebels, lack of consistent supplies to French forces, and disease combined to create the spectacle before Laussat's eyes in 1803. Paradoxically, the doctrine of liberty voiced by the rebels was quoted from the leaders of the French Revolution. This political philosophy, transplanted into the colonies and among the black slaves, sent shudders up the spines of the planters in lower Louisiana, to whom Laussat had to give frequent reassurances regarding France's *real* position on the issue of slavery. The First Consul was rumored to have made comments favorable to abolishing slavery, and Laussat's comments throughout the *Mémoires* reflect his own dilemma. Laussat wrote of Santo Domingo that French forces were

reduced to a very small number of troops who controlled the entire area, notably the plains. From the roadstead, the results of the destruction and pillaging could already be observed....Last Saturday the blacks attacked here. They failed to enter the town, but they burned its gates, the houses of d'Estaing, and the whole compound occupied by General Leclerc. Four or five days ago, the Negroes made a surprise attack on the isle of La Tortue, where we had our military hospitals. They slaughtered every human being there. The settler Labbatut [sic] was massacred and General Leclerc escaped in his shirt sleeves. Seeing the arrival of 350 soldiers, they made a final desperate attempt to take this point before the troops landed.

Journal, 66–67. Following this passage were pages of inventory regarding the land, produce, population, and trade in Santo Domingo, as submitted to Laussat by M. de Saint-Venant, a knowledgeable inhabitant. Journal, 74–86.

17   La Balise was a military post and pilot station situated some eighty-seven miles down the Mississippi River from New Orleans. Its unpretentious frame structures included a church, a commander's quarters, a guardhouse, a powder magazine, and a few barracks. Juan Ronquillo, the chief pilot, held a coveted monopoly on all piloting service from there into the Mississippi Delta. Because of sandbars, numerous invisible islets, floating obstacles, and contrary winds, experienced pilots were required for ships in the area that were on their way upriver to New Orleans. It was not uncommon for ships to be stalled there for weeks because of contrary winds.

18   Laussat notified Governor Salcedo of his arrival and requested a suitable reception in accordance with protocol. See letter in Archives nationales, Ser. C13A, vol. 52, 73.

19   Laussat wrote that the young officer "was de Bouligny. A young, well-born Creole, Louis de Bouligny, third son of the last colonel of the Louisiana Regiment, was accompanied by Girardais, Burthe, Vinache, Serre, Blanque." Deletion from *Mémoires* manuscript, 38. Such notes cited hereinafter as deletions from the *Mémoires* manuscript refer to manuscript material that Laussat chose not to have published in the 1831 version of *Mémoires sur ma vie.*

20   In his first reaction to Louisianians, Laussat wrote of his hosts: "His wife is a big woman, quite young. They have three sons and four daughters, one of whom is very beautiful and bears the name of Camille. [Laussat had a daughter of that name also.] Their oldest son is adjutant first pilot; the second, also a pilot, is the one who brought our brig into port; the third is a baby." Deletion from *Mémoires* manuscript, 42.

21   "Before boarding, M. Colson, a passenger on a ship ready to leave for Havana, came to see me. He is a merchant, a friend of Piton [James Pitot]....I am patiently awaited in New Orleans. The agents of the Spanish government are behaving like a moribund people. The Anglo-Americans in general are furious; those in the West shall be ours. We must foster this diversity of feelings and interests." Journal, 108.

22   Pierre Joseph de Favrot, a lieutenant colonel of militia, had the rank of brigadier general in command at Fort Saint-Philippe. He was also known as Don Pedro under the Spanish administration. On a list of important citizens in Louisiana, drawn up before the transfer of the colony to the United States, Laussat attached the following note to Favrot's name: "Creole, of grenadiers, rank of lieutenant colonel. Will take his retirement after the cession." Deletion from *Mémoires* manuscript, 42. A census of inhabitants residing along the Mississippi in 1803 exists in the Journal.

23 "He served us a breakfast of *café au lait*, eggs and pigeons." Deletion from *Mémoires* manuscript, 48.

24 "A great assembly of people was waiting for us there—among others, M. Charpin, a friend and administrator of the Pontalba estates; Mérieult, son-in-law of the Siblains; Albin Michel, my old acquaintance, who was also a brother of M. Barthèlemy and a son-in-law of the Mardats. They served a delicious dinner." Journal, 117. Among those mentioned above, Jean-François Mérieult was the merchant of New Orleans who built the property which is now 533 Royal Street, the present site of the Historic New Orleans Collection.

25 "At eleven o'clock, I went to the governor's mass with him and then accompanied him back to his residence. There I dined with him at three o'clock, in the company of the major commanders, the vicar-general, the head of the *cabildo*, and the merchant Faurie. Burthe, Vinache, Neurisse, and Daugerot had also been invited. Toasts were raised to the respective governments and to others. The rounds of drinks were endless." Deletion from *Mémoires* manuscript, 35. Laussat was soon to discover that the condescension of the Spanish officers, the zeal and apparent loyalty of the governor, and the eagerness to please on the part of the intendant, were all short-lived indeed.

26 "Citizen Charpin has been among the first to work for the formation of this company [a volunteer unit], which has brought honor to the French name on these shores; he was selected its captain. He is a retired soldier who counts several battle scars and thirty years of effective service, not including six campaigns. He only left the army in 1794 in order to reform the auxiliary battalion in the colonies where he was. He has always enjoyed the most remarkable esteem of his comrades and chiefs. He loves France with enthusiasm and jealousy; he gives proof of it here on all occasions." Letter from Laussat to Denis Decrès, 3 nivôse an XII (December 25, 1803) in the Laussat Papers.

27 Alexander O'Reilly was born near Dublin, Ireland, in 1722. He fled to Spain and joined an Irish brigade there. Having on one occasion saved the life of the king of Spain, Charles III, he was elevated to the rank of lieutenant general in the army. He arrived in New Orleans on July 24, 1769, as Spanish governor, with instructions to crush a revolt on the part of some Creoles, which he did. Laussat explained the results, therefore, of the publication of his proclamation: "The governor appeared displeased....He would have preferred that I address it to him alone as the head of the government here. He resented the fact that the proclamation was published and placarded while he was still governor....It made a salutary impression on all the settlers in the colony." Journal, 119. One can readily understand why the Spanish officials did not go out of their way after this incident to be "helpful" to Laussat in the performance of his duties.

28 Juan Ventura Morales was interim intendant during the term of Manuel Gayoso de Lemos as governor (1797–1799). The impolitic measure of clamping down on American river trade is attributed to him; however, Laussat seemed to produce reasons for putting the blame on Salcedo. Georges Oudard contends that Morales was a wicked person, sinister and a hater of the French, in *Vieille Amérique*, 265. Marc de Villiers du Terrage, on the other hand, credits him with great integrity, in *Louisiane française*, 468. After the cession of Louisiana, Morales went to Pensacola.

From there he went to Havana and finally to Puerto Rico, where he died in 1819. On the issue of the American claim to right of deposit, Laussat noted: "The *chargé d'affaires* of France in the United States, M. Pichon, informed me of the stir created in the United States at the suppression of the right of deposit in New Orleans as ordered by Morales, and he likewise informed me that President Jefferson had sent James Monroe to France to treat with our government about this critical situation." Journal, 120.

29   "In the afternoon, I held some long conferences, first, with the *alcalde* Lanusse regarding supplies, municipal affairs, and trade; second, with the intendant about admitting French colors into the port, about administration in the colony—its finances and revenues—and about certain individuals; and third, with the war commissioner regarding some police cases, notably, one concerning three prisoners of state." Journal, 122.

30   Laussat records this incident slightly differently on p. 123 of his Journal. His wife had already arrived at the church when the governor informed her "before the whole congregation" that the king himself walked on that day. As she was leaving the church, "she was challenged in the middle of the street by a black sentinel with a drawn bayonet," who said he was acting on orders from the officer of the guard.

31   In a questionnaire regarding social customs in Louisiana, Laussat observed the following:
      "It is a luxury to wear merchandise of a superior quality, without the glitter of gold and silver, imported from India, England, and France. The furniture is proper but English, although marble-top tables with gilded legs, large mirrors, clocks, etc., are brought in from France. There are few four-wheel carriages, but many two-wheel cabs, and several are brought in from France.
      Social and cultural life is as developed here as it is in Paris. The people are far more frank, docile, and sincere than in Europe. They are pleasant and very polite, and they give a general impression that delights the foreigners. There is a great deal of social life; elegance and good breeding prevail throughout. Domestics are ordinarily Negroes and mulattoes of both sexes. There are numerous hairdressers and all sorts of masters—dancing, music, art, and fencing, etc. All the people in New Orleans love to read. There are no book shops or libraries, but books are ordered from France." *Résponses sur la Louisiane*, in the Laussat Papers.

32   He sent the official messages and reports through Blanque. Letter from Laussat to Denis Decrès, 15 nivôse an XII (January 6, 1804), in Archives nationales, Ser. C13A, vol. 52, 2–3.

33   For a list of the existing posts in Louisiana in 1803, see the documents and reports in French and Spanish among the Laussat Papers.

34   The name *Attakapas* is frequently misspelled in the *Mémoires*. It is believed to have been an aboriginal term for 'man-eaters.' In 1803 Viel was the only native Louisianian to have entered the Society of Jesus. In 1792 he returned to Louisiana because of French anticlericalism.

35   Auguste Chouteau played a leading role, together with Pierre Leclède, in founding the city of Saint Louis.

36   For the exact descriptions on conditions in upper Louisiana, see the report of Auguste Chouteau to the colonial prefect of Louisiana, August 12, 1803, in the Laussat Papers.

37   Natchitoches was a post in which the occupants were engaged in min-

ing, growing tobacco, farming, and trading. At one time they had the ambition to rival Bordeaux in the manufacturing of wine.

38 The names Boré, Baure, and Borée all appear in the *Mémoires* and correspondence of Laussat, who was not careful about spelling. The person in question was Jean-Etienne de Boré de Mauleon. In a report, Laussat informed Decrès that in looking for a qualified person to fill the post of city mayor, he had his eye on "Boré, a Creole from a distinguished family, a former musketeer in France, one of the strongest and ablest planters of Louisiana, and a man well known for his patriotism and the unshakable independence of his character." Laussat to Denis Decrès, 20 frimaire an XII (December 12, 1803), in Laussat Papers, 4.

39 Francisco Luis Hector, baron de Carondelet, was governor of Louisiana (1792–1797). His term in office was closely identified with (1) plans to separate Kentucky from the United States in order to annex it to Spain; (2) the schemes of the French envoy, Edmond C. Genet, to organize during the mid-1790s a volunteer corps in Kentucky with which to invade Louisiana and Florida; and (3) negotiations with Spain for complete freedom of navigation on the Mississippi River. An able administrator and engineer, he succeeded in aborting insurrections, maintaining order and peace in the colony, and supporting a variety of public works projects.

40 Don Bernardo de Gálvez, Spanish governor of Louisiana (1777–1783), was later viceroy of Mexico. He was responsible for several successful campaigns against the English in the Gulf area during the American Revolution, and he encouraged economic development in the colony.

41 See the ad regarding the sale of Laussat's library in *Moniteur de la Louisiane*, No. 383 (February 18, 1804), 3. Since he would have to travel to Martinique under an assumed name to avoid the British, who blockaded the coasts, he was forced to sell most of his books in Louisiana. Several Laussat bookplates are among the items with the Laussat Papers.

42 Laussat approved slaves "with moderation" because he wished to maintain the support of the influential Louisiana slaveholders and because he himself had private interests in the traffic. Ignorant of steps to be taken by the United States on this matter and fearing that they might intitiate lenient measures too quickly, he issued a decree known as the Black Code on December 17, 1803—only three days before he transferred the colony to the United States.

43 The word *interprète* is marked out in the manuscript version and substituted with *truchman*, which means *go-between*. Fabre, therefore, acted not as a simple interpreter, but as an intermediary. Tappalca was the name given the Indian chief in the original manuscript and the Journal. Years later, Laussat corrected this to the right name, Tastiky. See Laussat, *Mémoires*, 133; Journal, 249–50. For Indian terms, see also William A. Read, *Louisiana-French* (Baton Rouge, La., 1931), 86–87. Spain's inability to control the widespread raiding activities of Seminole Indians, runaway slaves, and white outlaws prompted the Monroe administration to send General Andrew Jackson into East Florida to restore order in 1817–1818. Jackson's campaign resulted in the United States purchasing the area from Spain in 1819.

44 This period of confinement accounts for the hiatus in the manuscript between the dates of July 1 and July 25, 1803. Laussat noted on p. 289 of his Journal: "It is twenty-five days today since I have last written in my

Journal; it is twenty-four days now since I went to bed with the fever."
Yellow fever was acutely infectious because of the constant exposure of
humans to mosquitoes, which carried the virus. The disease was well
known throughout the subtropical and tropical climates of the New
World, and it contributed to the defeat of the French army in Santo
Domingo during Laussat's day. Later in the century it caused widespread devastation among Europeans and Americans attempting to con-
struct the Panama Canal. For a variety of medical reasons, the newly
arrived Europeans were particularly vulnerable to the disease.

45   In the manuscript version, reference to Burthe is made by the single
letter "B." The most information regarding Burthe is provided in his
pamphlet, *Burthe contre Laussat. Première partie. Louisiane, Ier janvier 1804,
10 nivóse, XIIe année républicaine.* (New Orleans, 1804), a copy of which
may be found in the Special Collections Division, Howard-Tilton Memorial Library at Tulane University. A brief account is found in: Simone
de la Souchère Deléry, *Napoleon's Soldiers In America* (Gretna, La., 1972),
19, 49–50.

46   "My public conduct had the full approbation of both the minister of the
navy and the First Consul of the government." Deletion from *Mémoires*
manuscript, 156. See also documents for mid-July among the Laussat
Papers.

47   "His brazen attitude and the part, open as well as clandestine, that he
played in the storm of abuse and in the escape of Candon finally ruined
him altogether before the authorities." Deletion from *Mémoires* manuscript, 156. The reference is to the assistance which Burthe gave to Captain Candon, who deserted his ship in the spring of 1804, contrary to
Laussat's orders, and who forcibly resisted arrest by the American authorities.

48   What Laussat implies here is that he did not wish to compromise himself
with the Spanish leaders before he was convinced that the negotiations
between their governments in Europe had been completed. He was not
officially installed as colonial prefect of the colony, and he therefore felt it
was not prudent to expose himself at this time by making statements at
official functions. General Victor, not Laussat, had been commissioned
to represent France at the ceremonies for the retrocession of Louisiana by
Spain. Hence, Laussat found himself in an awkward position: he was in
New Orleans occupying an official post, but without full powers, without the correct orders, and, above all, without military forces by which
he could have French interests fully respected by all parties. Bonaparte
issued Laussat's commission to represent France on June 6, 1803, and
these instructions and certificates reached Laussat in November. Only
then did he have the necessary credentials to negotiate officially with the
Spanish and American authorities regarding the particular details of the
successive transfers in sovereignty over Louisiana held on November 30
with Spain and on December 20 with the United States.
      Among the Laussat Papers is a report prepared by Captain Pierre
Landais, a military courier who brought the instructions from the French
government in Washington to Laussat in New Orleans. This document
is entitled "Journal de Baltimore à la Nouvelle-Orléans parterre"; or see
the synopsis provided by Robert D. Bush, "Voyage du Citoyen Landais à
Louisiane en 1803," *Revue de Louisiane*, V (Summer, 1976), 45–48.

49   "My wife is adjusting here marvelously; she devotes herself to instruc-

tive reading; she watches over the children and the household; she enlivens our family talks which are limited to Daugerot, Blanque, two or three other friends; from time to time she steps out to take a ride in her carriage." Deletion from *Mémoires* manuscript, 156.

50 Originally included as a footnote, the following table of market prices current in 1803 for the principal foodstuffs is given in the units of French currency, the franc and the centime. The franc in 1803 had a value of about twenty cents. The centime equals 1/100 of a franc and is abbreviated by the lower case letter *c*. For purposes of quickly converting values, consider fifty centimes as equal to ten cents. Another unit of currency used during Laussat's day was the piastre forte (Spanish), which was about equal to the American dollar. Later the gourd from Haiti was also used; it, too, had a value of about one dollar. Refugees from Santo Domingo frequently used this monetary unit in their transactions in Louisiana long after its transfer to the United States and even to statehood in 1812.

Bread, 1 pound	18 to 25 c.
Butcher's meat, per pound:	
from April to October	10 to 12 c.
from October to April	15 to 18 c.
Poultry, namely:	
table fowl, a pair	7 fr. 50c.
hens, a pair	5 fr. to 6 fr. 25c.
chickens, a pair	3 fr. 75c. to 5 fr.
capons, a pair	7 fr. 50c.
ducks, a pair	5 fr.
turkeys, a pair	20 fr.
young turkeys, a pair	12 fr. 50c.
goose or gosling, each	3 fr. 75c.
partridge or other game birds	1 fr. 25c. to 1 fr. 65c.
eggs, per dozen	1 fr. 25c. to 1 fr. 65c.
Trout, 1 pound	65c.
Eel, 1 pound	65c.
Redfish or perch, 1 pound	95c.

These fish come from the lake and are called "first-class". The common fish come from the river and are sold fresh by fishermen.

Oysters, per hundred	2 fr. 50c.
Fresh-water crawfish, per 20	60c.
Shrimp, per 30	60c.
Kale	90c.
Green beans, a small dish	90c.
Tomatoes, 15	60c.
Turnips, 6	30c.
Leeks, a small bunch	30c.
Havana bananas	3 fr. 15c.
Apples	60c.
Peaches, 4	60c.
Plums, a dish	60c.
Figs	60c.
Pomegranates, 2	30c
Corn, a barrel	15 fr.
Refined sugar (prime quality), 1 pound	1 fr. 80c.

Refined sugar (second grade), 1 pound	1 fr. 25c.
Clayed sugar, 1 pound	80c.
Native horses, regular	1,000 to 1,500 fr.
Carriage-horses, two assorted, of the Natchez variety	4,000 to 5,000 fr.

European goods were sold here at 50 to 100 percent more than the regular prices in France.

Fashioning of a:

suit	20 fr.
uniform	35 fr.
vest	10 fr.
pair of trousers	10 fr.

Tailors make these last two articles at 5 fr. each.

Rental prices for days of slave-labor and the type of work:

Slave coachman (driver), per month	90 fr.
Cook, per month	90 fr.
Assistant cook, per month	75 fr.
Servants, per month	75 fr.
Gardener	70 fr.
Farmhand, per month	50 fr.
Laundress, etc., per month	60 fr.

One gives slaves, in addition, their rations; nearly all of their clothing; and every Sunday, a bonus of 1 fr.50c. to 2 fr.50c.

Master carpenter, daily	10 fr.
Carpenter	10 fr.
Locksmith	10 fr.
Assistant laborer	6 fr. 25c.
Manual laborer	3 fr. 75c.
Female laborer	2 fr. 50c.

A slave contracts himself to bring a fixed sum to his master and keeps whatever he can earn over that amount.

The majority of the foremen are Europeans, and their workmen are either mulattoes or free blacks. There are some among the latter who are slaves but who are classed as an inferior rank.

51 Antoine Morin was a refugee from Santo Domingo. He attempted to dissuade Boré from his idea of substituting the production of sugar for that of indigo, but having failed, he joined him. Success was immediate. However, he soon moved his sheds elsewhere in Louisiana after dissolving his partnership with Boré.

52 He also introduced a system of small ditches worked by locks for controlled irrigation of the land.

53 In widespread use among American Indians, it was a game similar to hockey, though it did have local variations.

54 English and American newspapers and bulletins, as well as letters arriving in New Orleans from abroad, carried news of the Louisiana Purchase. One such notice dated July 4, 1803, is found in the Journal. It concerns the treaty signed in Paris on April 30. In spite of the notice published in the Philadelphia Gazette, August 11, 1803, which observed that Mr. King, former ambassador in London, had himself brought the news, Laussat refused to acknowledge it publicly. Official correspondence to Laussat on this subject, along with instructions from Pichon, did not reach Laussat until August 18, 1803.

BOOK TWO

1   The original crude process of crushing the sugarcane was by means of a mill wheel turned by four mules. Etienne Boré attributed his success to a devised system of irrigation by which water from the river could be conducted to his fields through a series of narrow ditches called canals, which could be controlled by small locks. By this system he was able to regulate more successfully the water content in the cane. From Etienne Boré's report on sugar manufacturing to Laussat (June 27, 1803), Laussat Papers. The juice usually registered between 7° and 11° on a Baumé hydrometer for saccharine richness, thus 8½° was quite normal.

2   The term *propre*, as well as *bagasse, vesou*, and *flambeau*, was a common expression used in describing the process of sugar refining. See: J. Carlyle Sitterson, *Sugar Country: The Cane Sugar Industry in the South, 1753–1950* (Lexington, Ky., 1953), 133–46.

3   Until 1803, an extensive amount of wood was consumed in the operations of sugar manufacturing. So the use of the dull-colored pulp was a fortuitous discovery. However, until its use by Destrehan, *bagasse* was not used in lower Louisiana simply because they had not yet found a way of extracting the water content from the cane stalks. By 1900, some English industrialists conceived the idea that this extract could serve as a suitable raw material in the process of paper manufacturing.

4   According to page 498 of the Journal, the name of the man was Lacoste.

5   Trépagnier was known to have been severe with his household. The account in the Journal tells us that he was wanted alone and at night, not at the door, but at a place far removed from the house.

    The Trépagnier plantation had a long and interesting history. It was a rich tract of land near Lake Pontchartrain, given to Trépagnier by the king of Spain for distinguished service. It then passed from his family to Richard Butler, who sold it to the Ormonds, who in turn sold it to McCutcheon, whose son, Samuel, married Adele d'Estrehan of the neighboring plantation. Later, the d'Estrehans sold it to the Henderson family. And so the land changed hands until it became the property of the American Oil Company, which, in 1971, donated the Destrehan Plantation House and four acres of land to the River Road Historical Society, now its exclusive owner.

6   The settlers always referred to the two sides of the river as "the coast" (côte), hence Côte des Allemands (German Coast) and Côtes des Acadiens (Acadian Coast).

7   Deletion from *Mémoires* manuscript, 20: Although he was a painter, he was primarily a musician.

8   Bringier was the first Louisianian to set up a general country store.

9   Bringier assumed the responsibility for maintaining a relay station, covering the cost of food and care for the horse. Like so many other early settlers in Louisiana, he had several different sources of income.

10 "His [Cantrille's] children go hunting with them and speak their language, a kind of Choctaw. These Indians speak French and their women have adopted European names and dress." Journal, 543.

11 The batture is a small tongue of land that serves as a defense against the continual movement of the waters and preserves the foundation of the land. The anse is detrimental; it refers to the continual washing of waters that gouges deeper and deeper into the silt deposits of the riverbed.

12   One married into the Mandeville family; another into the de Marigny family—her husband was a grandfather to Bernard de Marigny; and a third married into the Arnauld family.

13   While serving in the American army as its commander in chief, James Wilkinson received some rewards from the Spanish government for informing them about American plans. He exaggerated his own role as a military man, and such dreams of grandeur led him to become implicated in the abortive conspiracy of Aaron Burr in 1806. See the account of these turbulent years by James Wilkinson, *Memoirs of My Own Time* (3 vols.; Philadelphia, 1816), I.

14   One senses here a tone of bitter disappointment. The assignment came as keen disillusionment. He was assigned to serve as second in administration under the captain general.

15   Since he was preparing the list for printing, Laussat was most careful to choose words that would not compromise him in any way. He marked out *Il me fallait* and substituted it with *Je me proposais*. Notes in parentheses are from the Journal, 625-27. See the original proclamation among the Laussat Papers.

16   Laussat at this point washed his hands of the complicated and mutually contradictory boundary disputes regarding the frontiers of Louisiana, particularly the West Florida dispute between Spain and the United States, which would drag on for more than a decade. Laussat was equally uncooperative with the Americans on this issue. He bluntly told Claiborne and Wilkinson that such matters were between their government and Spain's, since he had merely transferred to the United States what the Spanish had given to him, complete with all of the boundary disputes. See relevant documents and correspondence with William C.C. Claiborne and James A. Wilkinson in Laussat Papers.

17   Bearing in mind, no doubt, the motive of Spain—to prevent the annexation of Louisiana to the United States at any cost, by force if need be—Laussat had no other choice. Pichon had been very explicit in his letters:

> The dispatches from Paris announce that this power [Spain] has made known its displeasure over the cession of Louisiana to the United States. It does not appear that these dispositions have been voiced by a formal opposition, otherwise I would have surely been informed of it. Nevertheless, the Spanish minister [Marquis de y Riujo in Washington] either because he is executing or exaggerating his instructions, has taken steps which lead one to fear that, while circumspect in Paris, the court in Madrid may have given to New Orleans orders contrary to those of the month of October—orders that produce a refusal to turn the colony over to you. Not only does the Marquis d'Yrujo protest against the acquisition by the United States, but he even presses them not to accomplish the [terms of the] treaty by the payment of stipulated compensations. And what is no less significant, he has refused to certify the copy of the documents, both Spanish and French, which will authorize you to require the return of Louisiana from the Spanish officials.
>
> As it will be urgent to have no further doubts about it as soon as possible, I have determined, without waiting for the exchange of ratifications, to expedite [the transmission of] the orders to you for taking possession in the name of the French government, without the refusal and the subterfuges of the Spanish minister; they should be on the way.

The sole motive provided by the government for taking possession only on the very day that they turn it over to the Americans is the fear of England; but that power has formally and by public notification acquiesced to the cession to the United States, and we are sure that that danger is no longer to be apprehended.

Letter from Pichon to Laussat, 11 vendémaire an XII (October 13, 1803), in the Laussat Papers, 2-3.

Then, nine days later, in another dispatch from Pichon, Laussat was told:

The intention of the government, Citizen . . . was at first that the possession should be taken in the name of France on the same day that the deliverance would be made to the United States. That arrangement, as I have pointed out to you, was established upon a fear lest England, during the interim of the two transactions, seize Louisiana. Today this fear is groundless; consequently, it is extremely important to ascertain the dispositions of the Spanish officers and the point to which the steps of the minister of that country here are linked with counterorders given in New Orleans. On the other hand, if the orders of the month of October, 1802, still hold, it is important to take formal possession and in that way obviate any eventualities.

I think, Citizen, I am able to advise you—and this advice is in accord with the American government—to present yourself before the Spanish commanders with the purpose of taking possession. If they are disposed to give it up, you will have the forts evacuated, you will have delivered to you such a symbol of sovereignty as you judge most manifest, and you will have the acts and the minutes of the delivery exacted by the instructions of the respective governments, signed....If, on the contrary, Citizen, the Spanish authorities refuse to deliver the colony, it will be advisable perhaps to make a protest and wait for the time when the ratification of the United States being given, these latter shall send their commissioner. You shall then transfer the order of taking possession from the First Consul to that commissioner, and probably that would be the most regular manner of executing the treaty in favor of the United States, against the opposition of the Spanish officials.

Pichon to Laussat, 20 vendémaire an XII (October 22, 1803), in the Laussat Papers.

18   Only one American refused—Benjamin Morgan, who considered himself disqualified for his post because he knew not one word of French or Spanish.

In another closed meeting with his immediate subordinates—Vinache, Costille, Dusseuil, and Allier, among others—Laussat gave directives and sought to inspire a sense of courage and determination in them. He needed to destroy an initial uncertainty and timidity which these men felt in their new roles in public service. Allier was then captain of the port of New Orleans.

19   "We agreed that we would call on them when needed and that during the ceremonies they would be prepared and ready for any eventuality." Journal, 639.

20 The walk to city hall was "with Vinache on my right, Costille on my left, then Dusseuil, Daugerot, and Blanque, my faithful friend. Although in bourgeois dress, standing with military bearing were also Charpin and about fifty Frenchmen—Neurisse, Albin, Camut... Legrand, Malry, Baritot, Ducourneau, Segur, and many others." Journal, 639–40.

21 This dance is performed by a specified number of dancers. The first couple executes the steps and is then followed by a number of partners who take up the steps and continue the round. The *contredanse*, like the quadrille, is lively and light, with gentlemen and ladies executing the steps facing each other.

22 The term *citoyen* was associated initially with the radical (anti-monarchist, anti-clerical) phases of the French Revolution, hence it was not accidental that opposition to such usage in Louisiana surfaced. Use of *citoyen* by Saint-Julien in 1803 must have been somewhat comparable to that of using the modern term *comrade* during the 1920s—both had become politicized during their respective eras.

23 Commanders of the posts or districts in December 1803:
    1. Première Côte des Allemandes: Antoine Armand, captain of the militia
    2. Seconde Côte des Allemands: Manuel Andry, captain of the militia
    3. Cabahonace: Michel Cantrille, lieutenant of the army, captain of the militia
    4. Valenzuela or Lafourche des Chatinachas: Raphael Roquin, lieutenant of the Louisiana Regiment
    5. Côte d'Iberville: François Rivas, captain;
    6. Galveston: Thomas Estevan, lieutenant of the Louisiana Regiment
    7. Pointe-Coupée: Guillaume Duparc, captain of the army and lieutenant.
In the Journal, 673–74.

24 The *ambigu* is a cold collation taken between lunch and dinner, or between dinner and late evening, at which the dishes served must be cold, and at which all the dishes—sweet courses as well as the dessert—are served at the same time. *Ambigu* is also a night meal—a supper served at an evening party between midnight and two o'clock in the morning.

25 The verbatim text of the letter from Fort Adams (December 7, 1803), is as follows:

The commissioners on the part of the United States for receiving the Province of Louisiana.
To Citizen Laussat, colonial prefect, Commissioner of the French Government.
Sir, We hasten to acknowledge your welcome annunciation of the 30th which we have received a few minutes since, and, with lively emotions of joy, felicitate you on the transfer of the Province of Louisiana, from the government of Spain, to that of the French Republic; which we consider the precursor to the fulfillment of the Treaty of the 30th April, between our respective nations.
We shall embark tomorrow, and will advance with all the practicable diligence to take upon us the important charge, which has devolved on you, and to consummate an event which, we flatter ourselves, may seal the good understanding and perpetuate the amicable intercourse of Sister-republiks;

We have the honor to be with high consideration and respect your obedient servants.

[signed] William C.C. Claiborne
J. A. Wilkinson

In the Laussat Papers.

26 Vinache, Bellechasse, and Blanque were sent to meet Claiborne and Wilkinson. At these interviews Henri Molier served as interpreter for Laussat, and Decius Wadsworth for Claiborne and Wilkinson

27 In reporting the details of the cession of Louisiana to the United States, Laussat wrote that: "New Orleans alone will provide a million piastres (five million francs) within four years." Laussat to Denis Decrès, 3 nivôse an XII (December 25, 1803), in the Laussat Papers. See also, the letter of 30 pluviôse an XII (February 20, 1804), *pour son Excellence seule,* Laussat Papers.

28 *Ecarté* is a game of cards similar to triumph, and *bête* is a card game played like the French game *mouche.* *Médiateur* is a card game played by four persons with a whole deck of cards. The 10s, 9s, and 8s are removed. *Bouillots* is a game commonly played in the French salons of the time. The bouillot table of Laussat still forms part of the salon furnishing in the home of Antoine de Pré de Saint-Maur.

29 For example, one document, dated December 28, 1803, stated:

Sir, we have received your letter of the 24th Dec. 1803 and have been prevented by incessant occupation, from answering it earlier.

We are happy to learn that measures are in agitation, to give us satisfaction, respecting the possession of the several objects ceded by France to the United States, by the treaty of the 30th April [1803], and take great pleasure in observing the progress of those measures.

But we think proper to state, to you, our entire difference of opinion, with respect to the occupancy of the military posts of Louisisana.

We deem it to be incontrovertible, that the evacuation of a military post implies the surrender of everything essential to its defense, and therefore we cannot admit that we have been put in complete possession, so long as the guard-houses are occupied by the guards, the barracks by the troops, the store-houses by the ammunitions and effects, and the hospitals by the sick of Spain; and more especially, while the keys of the powder magazines of Fort St. Charles and Fort St. Louis, remain in the hands of the agents and officers of the Spanish crown.

Feeling, however, an unwillingness to press this subject further, we content ourselves, at present, with a declaration of the claims of the United States and hasten to give you assurance of the readiness with which we shall accede to any practicable arrangement, for the general accomodation of all concerned. In the meantime, feeling persuaded of the good dispositions of the commissioner of France, to the United States, and of his zeal for the prompt execution of the treaty, we rest in confidence that this inconvenience and obstacle, encountered by the troops of the United States, will be remedied as speedily as circumstances will permit.

Be pleased to accept the assurance of our high consideration and respect.

[signed] William C. C. Claiborne
J. A. Wilkinson

In the Laussat Papers.

30   The posts in question were: St. Louis, Illinois, Nouvelle Bourbon, Ste.-Génèvieve, Cap Girardeau, Nouvelle Madrid, Arkansas, Natchitoches, Quachitas, Rapides, Camp or Fort de l'Espérance, and Avoyelles.

31   "In spite of her advanced pregnancy, my wife was gay and charming." Deletion from *Mémoires* manuscript, 104. See also the "Portrait de Madame Laussat" in *Moniteur de la Louisiane*, No. 377 (January 7, 1804), in the Archieves nationales, Ser. C13A, fols. 53, 123. Other deleted recollections of his family are as follows:

>   My wife's delicate pregnancy is quite painful. The day before yesterday, she was moaning on her bed. Zoë was not sleeping. She rose in her nightgown and, sobbing, came and leaned against the head of the bed. "Now what's wrong with you?" her mother said to her. "Ah, mamma, I'm all right. But you are suffering. I can't sleep." We had no end of trouble getting her back to bed. She has recovered quite well. She reasons, talks, and behaves like an angel. Sophie is unspoiled and a little inclined to quibble. Her cheerfulness and her sallies of wit and temperament amuse us. She is neither reserved nor resentful, but is obstinate and affectionate. She loves to tease and is, in all, a good child. Camille is sensitive, endearing, sensible, anxious to please, and jealous of her duties.

Deletion from *Mémoires* manuscript, 123.

32   This insistent carping on the Americans, particularly certain officials, in his letters to his superiors and to his family and friends was Laussat's undoing. It may have been the reason behind Bonaparte's final decision against appointing him to replace Pichon in Washington. What Laussat seemed not to have realized was that he was exonorating himself and the French people at the expense of the reputation of the American people. His marked dislike for anything American runs like a red thread throughout his writings. The French minister in Washington was concerned, and he asked Laussat to moderate his personal prejudices and try to get along more amicably with the American agents in the interest of Franco-American relations.

33   Wounded French officers and soldiers came from Saint-Nicholas, Mole, as did a detachment of French troops, women, and children fleeing from the vicinity of Anglo-French military engagements in the West Indies. This group of refugees sought asylum in a neutral territory. "Charity," wrote Claiborne, "enjoins us not to refuse them a temporary residence and humanity calls upon us to contribute to their relief; but the obligation of Neutrality renders it indispensable that they depart as soon as possible. This line of conduct is required by the laws of nations in terms too explicit to be misunderstood and sanctioned by the uniform practice of neutral powers." Letter to Laussat, January 27, 1804, in Laussat Papers.
   On board ship were 9 officers, 20 junior officers, and 36 soliders—65 military combatants in all. There were also 6 pharmacists, 1 hospital director, 2 staff officers, 23 nurses (major), some regular nurses, 13 women, 2 passengers, and 13 sailors forming the crew. In all there was a total of about 119 persons. Journal, 850–53.

34   Letter from William C. C. Claiborne and James A. Wilkinson to Laussat, March 26, 1804, in Laussat Papers.

35   If his actions were useful to his country, they certainly did little to foster amicable relations between France and the United States. His last letter to Pichon and also to his superiors in Paris contained derogatory remarks

and sharp criticisms of Claiborne, Wilkinson, Clark, and all who, so he thought, deprived him of whatever ambitions he had nurtured for his future in Louisiana.

36   His first impulse dictated "quitter" as the proper word to use here, then he crossed it over heavily and wrote *m'en separer*. Laussat did not feel he was leaving Louisiana freely but that he was being forcibly separated from it. Journal, 953.

37   "The carriage will wait for me behind the Marigny sawmill next to my house. Daugerot will come along." Journal, 952. Laussat departed from Louisiana to Martinique under the assumed name of Pierre Lanthois. His passport carries this information: "Lanthois (Jean) and Pitot Co., a refugee from St. Dominique and a naturalized citizen of the United States." In the Laussat Papers.

38   A traditional Béarnais luncheon consisting of homemade bread rubbed generously with lard and garlic and washed down with a beverage.

39   In the preface to the fourth book of Part One of the manuscript version of his *Mémoires*, Laussat made this final observation:

> By presenting in this way the results of my administration, I deprive myself of the occasion to bring forward my zeal, my fidelity, my greater or lesser ability to fulfill the views and intentions of the government that had chosen me to try out, in this colony, some of the experiments applicable to others. I am not developing the wisdom and legality of the means I employed, or the obstacles and the intrigues that I had to surmount, or the firmness with which I was obliged constantly to arm myself, or, finally, in that perpetual sequence of contrarieties, the constant irreprehensibility of my conduct. I say flatly, "This is what I have done. Laugh, if you dare—my works answer for me."

Bibliography

Archival Collections and Personal Libraries consulted:
Historic New Orleans Collection archives.
Les archives départmentales de Béarn à Pau, France.
Les archives nationales de la marine á Paris, France.
Louisiana Historical Society Library, at the Cabildo, New Orleans.
Louisiana State Archives, Baton Rouge.
Louisiana State Museum Archives, at the Cabildo, New Orleans.
Papers of the countess Hélène de Bar de la Garde, Bordeaux, France.
Papers of the viscount d'Origny, Paris, France.
Personal papers of Antoine du Pré de Saint-Maur, Pau, France.
Special Collections Division, Howard-Tilton Memorial Library, Tulane University, New Orleans.

Published Works:
Arthur, Stanley Clisby, *Old Familes of Louisiana*. Louisiana Classic Series. Baton Rouge: Claitor's, 1971.
Barbé-Marbois, François. *Histoire de la Louisiane et de la cession de cette colonie par la France aux Etats-Unis de l'Amérique septentrionale: précédée d'un discours sur la constitution et gouvernement des Etats-Unis*. Paris: Firmin Didot, 1829.
Baure, Faguet de. *Essais historiques sur le Béarn*. Paris: Denugon, 1818.
Bowles, William Augustus. *Authentic Memoirs of William Augustus Bowles, Esquire, Ambassador from the United Nations of Creeks and Cherokees to the Court of London*. London: R. Faulder, 1791.
Burthe, André. *Burthe contre Laussat. Première partie. Louisiane, Ier janvier 1804, 10 nivôse, XIIe année republicaine*. New Orleans: Beleurgey et Renard, 1804.
Bush, Robert D. "Colonial Administration in French Louisiana: The Napoleonic Episode, 1802–1803." *Publications of the Louisiana Historical Society*. 2nd ser., II (1975), 36–59.
————."Documents on the Louisiana Purchase: The Laussat Papers." *Louisiana History*, XVIII (Winter, 1977), 104–107.
————."Voyage du citoyen Landais à Louisiane en 1803." *Revue de Louisiane*, V (Summer, 1976), 45–48.
Carter, Clarence E., ed. *Territorial Papers of the United States, The Territory of Orleans, 1803–1812*. Vol. IX, Washington, D.C.: Government Printing Office, 1940.
Correspondance de Napoléon Ier. 32 vols. Paris: H. Plon, 1858–1870.
DeConde, Alexander. *This Affair of Louisiana*. New York: Charles Scribner's Sons, 1976.
Deléry, Simone de la Souchère. *Napoleon's Soldiers In America*. Gretna, La.: Pelican, 1972.
Douglas, Elisha P. "The Adventurer Bowles." *William and Mary Quarterly*. 2nd ser., VI (1949), 3–23.
Fletcher, Mildred S. "Louisiana as a Factor in French Diplomacy from 1763 to 1803." *Mississippi Valley Historical Review*, XVII (December, 1930), 367–76.
Fortier, Alcée. *History of Louisiana*. 4 vols. New York: Manzi, Jouant, 1904.

Gayarré, Charles. *History of Louisiana*. 4 vols. New Orleans: James Gresham, 1879.

Hatfield, Joseph T. *William Claiborne: Jeffersonian Centurion in the American Southwest*. Louisiana History Series. Lafayette: University of Southwestern Louisiana Press, 1976.

Kinnaird, Lawrence. "The Significance of William Augustus Bowles' Seizure of Panton's Apalachee Store in 1792." *Florida Historical Quarterly*, IX (1931), 156–92.

Krebs, Albert. "Laussat préfet de la Louisiane (19 août 1802–21 avril 1804)." *Bulletin de l'Institute Napoléon*. XLVIII (July, 1953), 65–72.

Lacaze, Louis. *Les imprimeurs et les libraires en Béarn, 1552–1883*. Pau, France: Leon-Ribaut, Impr., 1884.

Lafargue, André. "Pierre Clément de Laussat, Colonial Prefect and High Commissioner of France in Louisiana: His Memoirs, Proclamations, and Orders." *Louisiana Historical Quarterly*, XX (January, 1937), 159–82.

————."Pierre Clément de Laussat: An Intimate Portrait." *Louisiana Historical Quarterly*, XXIV (January, 1941), 5–8.

Laussat, Pierre Clément de. *Mémoires sur ma vie à mon fils, pendant les années 1803 et suivantes, que j'ai rempli des fonctions publiques, savoir: à la Louisiane, en qualité de commissaire du gouvernement français pour la reprise de possession de cette colonie et pour la remise aux Etats-Unis*. Pau, France: E. Vignancour, 1831.

Lepsy, V. and P. Raymond. *Dictionnaire béarnais: ancien et moderne*. 2 vols. Montpellier, France: Centrale du Midi, 1887.

Lyon, E. Wilson. *Bonaparte's Proposed Louisiana Expedition*. Chicago: private edition, distributed by the University of Chicago libraries, 1934.

————. *Louisiana in French Diplomacy, 1759–1804*. Norman: University of Oklahoma Press, 1934.

————.*The Man Who Sold Louisiana: The Career of François Barbé-Marbois*. Norman: University of Oklahoma Press, 1942.

McDermott, John Francis, ed. *Frenchmen and French Ways in the Mississippi Valley*. Urbana: University of Illinois Press, 1969.

————. *The French in the Mississippi Valley*. Urbana: University of Illinois Press, 1963.

Oudard, George. *Vieille Amérique: la Louisiane au temps des français*. Paris: H. Plon, 1931.

Read, William A. *Louisiana-French*. Baton Rouge: Louisiana State University Press, 1931.

Robertson, James Alexander. *Louisiana Under the Rule of Spain, France, and the United States*. 2 vols. Cleveland: Arthur H. Clark, 1911.

Sitterson, J. Carlyle. *Sugar Country: The Cane Sugar Industry in the South, 1753–1950*. Lexington: University of Kentucky Press, 1953.

Smith, Ronald D. "Napoleon and Louisiana: Failure of the Proposed Expedition to Occupy and Defend Louisiana, 1801–1803." *Louisiana History*, XII (Winter, 1971), 21–40.

Terrage, Marc de Villiers du. *Les Dernières Années de la Louisiane française*. Paris: Librairie Orientale et Américaine, 1903.

Tinker, Edward L. "Louisiana Changes Flags: The Tribulations of a Préfet Colonial." *Légion d'Honneur Magazine*, IX (1939), 375–84.

Wilkinson, James. *Memoirs of My Own Times*. 3 vols. Philadelphia: Abraham Small, 1816.

Wilson, Samuel, Jr. *Louisiana Purchase: An Exhibition Prepared by the Louisiana State Museum in Co-operation with the Louisiana Landmarks Society*. New Orleans: The Cabildo, 1953.

Index

sition of, 90, 127*n*20; during *Telegraph* affair, 93
Concordat, 5
Côte-des-Acadiens, 64, 124*n*6
Côte-des-Allemands, 82, 124*n*6
Creek Indians, 36–37
Creoles, 13, 59, 65, 100
Courier service, 66–67
Cuba, 9, 10, 106–107

Daugerot, Joseph, 79, 88–89
Davis, Samuel, 95, 96
Dayton, Jonathan, 33–35
Decrès, Denis, 114*n*2, 3; 116*n*9; 118*n*26; 119*n*32; 120*n*38
deLogny, Robin, 59, 73
Derbigny, Pierre, 75, 83, 92
d'Estrehan, Jean-Noel, 22, 60–61, 75
d'Estrépy, Pierre Marie Cabaret, 59
Donaldson, William, 76
Ducaila, Blanquet, 41
Dunmore, Lord, 36
Dupard, François, 64, 71—72, 127*n*7
Duplantier, Allard, 66
Duplessis plantation, 16
Duralde, Martin, 82, 84
Dusseuil, Lieutenant, 28, 89

Eboulis, 63–64, 71
England: and Anglo-French hostilities, 33, 56, 96; and Anglo-American rivalry, 56; Santo Domingo refugees and, 56; Acadians and, 64; commercial activity of, in the Floridas, 65–66; blockades Martinique, 108 *passim;* fears opposition to transfer, 125–26*n*17; mentioned, 42

Farnuel, Pierre, 29–32 *passim*
Faurie, Joseph, 32, 74, 76, 92
Favrot, Pierre Joseph de, 117*n*22. *See also* Plaquemines Fort
Fleuriau, Charles Jean, 73
Florida, 91, 98–99, 125*n*. *See also* Bowles, William Augustus
Folch, Vincente, y Juan, 81, 96
Forbes, John, 36, 38
Fort Bourbon, 15
Fort Duquesne, 35
Fort Saint Charles, 79
Fort Saint John, 81
Fort Saint Louis, 79

Fort Saint Philippe. *See* Plaquemines Fort
Fortier, Honoré, 103
Fortier, "la mère", 59, 70
Fortier, Michel, II, 52, 76, 92
France: military expedition of, in Louisiana, 21; 113–15*n;* and war with England, 42, 49; mentioned, 3, 32. *See also* Louisiana Purchase; Spanish colonies; United States
Fulton, Robert, 24

Gálvez, Don Bernardo de, 25, 120*n*40
Gaudin, Bonaventure, 65
Gauthier, Citizen, 94, 95
Gazette gouvernemental de la Nouvelle-Orléans, 74
Genet, Edmond C., 120*n*39
Gentilly plantation, 16
German settlement, 62, 63, 64, 66
Glopion, Catherine-Sophie de, 63
Guadeloupe, 108–109

Habine, Louis, 20
Hasset, Thomas, 84
Hazeur brothers, 52–53
Helvoët-Sluys, port of, 3, 32
Hevia, José Bernardo, 37
Hottinger & Cie, 33

Indians. *See* Cabahonacés; Choctaws; Creeks; Houmas; Osages; Seminoles; Topalcas

Jackson Square. *See* Place d'Armes
Jacobins, 43
Jefferson, Thomas, 80
Jones, Evan, 75

Labatut, Jean-Baptiste, 32, 76
Labatut, Jean-Baptiste, Santo Domingo, 9
La Balise pilot station: 11, 12–14 *passim*, 29, 97, 106, 117*n*17
Laclède, Pierre, 22, 119*n*35
Lafourche Parish, 64
Lake Pontchartrain, 25, 27
La Loutre pass, 12
Landais, Pierre, 73, 74, 121*n*48
Lanusse, Paul, 17, 32
La Tortue Island, Santo Domingo, 9
Laussat, Marie-Anne Peborde de, 3,

Ormond plantation, 60
Osage Indians, 22
Ossorne, Joaquim, 38
Ouachitas region, 23

Pain, Daniel, 69–70
Palao, Don Pedro Palas y Pratz, 26
Panton, WIlliam, 36 *passim*, 38
Parishes. *See* individual names of
Pau, France, 7
Pensacola: commercial relations with
    Louisiana, 36; Spanish troops de-
    part for, 103; mentioned, 27. *See
    also* Panton, William
Petit-Bourg, Guadeloupe, 108
Petit-Cavelier, Antoine Joseph, 75
Pichon, Louis André, 56–57, 73
Piernas, Don Pedro, 84
Pitot, James, 101
Pittsburgh, 35–36
Place d'Armes, 78–88 *passim*
Plaquemines Fort, 15, 29, 96, 106
Poey, Simon, 29, 30
Poeyferré, Jean Baptiste, 67
Point-a-Pitre, Guadeloupe, 108
Pointe-Coupée Parish, 22, 23, 40, 68,
    73
Pontalba, Joseph-Xavier Delfau de,
    18, 73
Posts: description of, 21, 91; com-
    manders appointed to, by Laussat,
    127n23
Poydras, Julien, 22
Premier alcalde, 17, 19
Priests, 19, 61–62, 67
New Providence Island, British West
    Indies, 36 *passim*, 106–107
Prudhomme, Emmanuel, 23

Relf, Richard, 93
Renaud, René, 56
Right of Deposit, 29. *See also*
    Morales, Juan Ventura
Rochefort, 3, 43
Roman, Jacques-Etienne, 22, 82
Ronquillo, Juan, 13–14, 117n17
Rousseau, Pierre-Georges, 37

Saint Charles Parish, 61
Saint John the Baptist Parish, 63
Saint-Julien, Pierre, 82–84
Saint-Marc-des-Apalaches, 37, 38
Saint Pé, Pierre, 73

Salcedo, Don Manuel, 15, 39
Salcedo, Don Manuel Juan de,
    (Spanish governor): description
    of, 13, 16, 19, 25, 79; right of depo-
    sit controversy and, 29; during re-
    trocession, 78–79
San Ildefonso Treaty, 76
Santander, 4–7
Santo Domingo: Laussat's arrival at,
    8; Negro rebellion in, 8–9, 116–
    17n16, influence in Louisiana, 18,
    55–56
Sarpy, Delord, 44
Sauvé, Pierre, 28, 75
Sawmills, 16, 72
Seminole Indians, 36, 38. *See also*
    Bowles, William Augustus
Siben, F. J., 17, 51
Solis, Manuel, 51
Someruelos, Salvador Muro y
    Salazar, marquis de, 20, 29, 116n9
Sorel, Joseph, 83
Spanish colonies: clergy in, 5–6, 19,
    61–62, 84; anti-French attitudes in,
    18, 19, 45–46, 76, 77–78, 83; admin-
    istration of, 19, 20, 74, 77–78,
    82–83, 101–102
Sugar manufacturing: description of,
    51–52, 59, 60–61, 70, 124n1, 3

Tafia, 51, 62
Tastiki, 39–40
Telegraph affair, 93 *passim*
Terre aux Boeufs Parish, 49
Tertulia, 5
Topalca Indians, 39
Trepagnier family, 62, 124n5
Tureaud, Augustine Dominique, 65,
    76

Ulloa, Don Antonio de, 13, 14
United States of America: expan-
    sionism of, described, 23, 24–25,
    66–67, 91, 98–99; immigration
    from, into Mississippi and Ohio
    valleys, 24–25, 36; right of deposit
    controversy and, 29; specific inter-
    est in, by Dayton, 33–35; Laussat's
    views of, 92–96, 100; and interest
    in the Floridas, 98–99; mentioned,
    74, 87, 89, 99. *See also* Commis-
    sioners